What people a‍ ‍ ‍ ‍ ‍ ‍ ‍ ‍ ‍ ‍ ‍ ‍ ‍ ‍ ‍out

Christoph‍

Burgis offers a fascinating and ... ife, work, and political views of Christopher Hitchens. ... e to come across a book that manages to combine an enjoyable and informative mix of history, philosophy, religion, and biography. Burgis accomplishes this difficult task well, and also helps the reader to interpret today's political climate.

**Ana Kasparian**, host and executive producer at The Young Turks

People who think Christopher Hitchens was god-like will be pissed. People who think Christopher Hitchens was nothing but a war-mongering scumbag will be pissed. For the rest of us, who loved Hitch but thought him deeply flawed, *Christopher Hitchens: What He Got Right, How He Went Wrong, and Why He Still Matters* is gold.

**Ed Buckner**, President, American Atheists (2008-2010) and Executive Director, Council for Secular Humanism (2001-2003)

Ben Burgis is invaluable to the socialist movement, not only because he has the ability to speak beyond the already converted, but because of his range and intellectual curiosity. His book on Hitchens shows this range, giving a fair analysis of a man who badly lost his bearings.

**Bhaskar Sunkara**, editor and publisher, *Jacobin* magazine

Ben Burgis has written a compelling account of the political and philosophical thought of Christopher Hitchens. Though many on the left would rather forget Hitchens, who in the last decade of his life made a decidedly imperialist turn, Burgis reveals that Hitchens remains an important thinker with whom anyone interested in the history of ideas should wrestle. An important book that will no doubt serve as a starting point for the many books likely to be written about Hitchens in coming years.

**Daniel Bessner**, Non-Resident Fellow at the Quincy Institute for Responsible Statecraft and Joff Hanauer Honors Associate Professor in Western Civilization at the University of Washington

This is a must read for anyone on the Left who admired Christopher Hitchens but wondered what the hell happened to him in the last decade or so of his life. With his characteristic rigor, clarity, and wit, Burgis offers a persuasive account of Hitch's evolution from young Trotskyist to neocon.

What is perhaps most impressive about this book—both its subject and its author—is the range on display. Burgis is happy to meet Hitchens on any field, whether it's the invasion of Iraq, a materialist critique of Said's Orientalism, or the intricacies of the Kalām cosmological argument for God's existence.

**Mark Warren**, Assistant Professor of Philosophy, Daemen College

Written in his trademark deliberative style, Ben Burgis' book is an engaging and worthwhile excavation of a writer now largely known for the reactionary turn he took in the final decade of his life. With care and thoroughness, Burgis offers us a more complete portrait of Christopher Hitchens' vast body of work — and mounts a compelling case that the best of it is still worth reading today.

**Luke Savage**, Author, *The Dead Center*, Bylines in *The Atlantic* and Staff Writer for *Jacobin* magazine

# Christopher Hitchens

What He Got Right, How He Went
Wrong, and Why He Still Matters

# Christopher Hitchens

## What He Got Right, How He Went Wrong, and Why He Still Matters

### Ben Burgis

Winchester, UK
Washington, USA

JOHN HUNT PUBLISHING

First published by Zero Books, 2021
Zero Books is an imprint of John Hunt Publishing Ltd., No. 3 East St., Alresford,
Hampshire SO24 9EE, UK
office@jhpbooks.com
www.johnhuntpublishing.com
www.zero-books.net

For distributor details and how to order please visit the 'Ordering' section on our website.

Text copyright: Ben Burgis 2021

ISBN: 978 1 78904 745 5
978 1 78904 746 2 (ebook)
Library of Congress Control Number: 2021947886

A CIP catalogue record for this book is available from the British Library.

Design: Stuart Davies

UK: Printed and bound by CPI Group (UK) Ltd, Croydon, CR0 4YY
Printed in North America by CPI GPS partners

We operate a distinctive and ethical publishing philosophy in
all areas of our business, from our global network of authors to
production and worldwide distribution.

# Contents

**Also by the Author**

*Give Them an Argument*, Zero Books,
ISBN: 978-1-78904-210-8

*Cancelling Comedians While the World Burns*, Zero Books,
ISBN: 978-1-78904-574-5

**With Matt McManus, Marion Trejo-McManus and Conrad
Bongard Hamilton**

*Myth and Mayhem*, Zero Books,
ISBN: 978-1-78904-553-6

Dedicated to the eternal memory of Michael Brooks, who encouraged me to write about Hitchens. I loved him like a brother and none of this is ever going to be as much fun without him.

**Chapter One**

# Christopher Hitchens vs. Bill and Hillary Clinton, Mother Teresa, Henry Kissinger, and God

Christopher Hitchens died of a complication of his esophageal cancer in 2011. Five years later, Hillary Clinton ran for president. Before somehow managing to lose to a racist and frequently incoherent reality television host in the general election, Clinton came shockingly close to losing the race for the Democratic nomination. The opponent who won 22 states and reshaped American politics was a protest candidate who looked like Doc Brown from *Back to the Future* and called himself a democratic socialist.

Many of Bernie Sanders' most ardent supporters were so young that, if they were familiar with "Hitch" at all, they may have only been familiar with a handful of YouTube videos from the final decade of his life where he uses his considerable rhetorical skills to embarrass Christian apologists in debates about atheism. They might not have guessed that Hitchens had spent most of his adult life as a committed socialist.

Just before the end of Bill Clinton's presidency, Hitchens came out with a book called *No One Left to Lie To: The Values of the Worst Family* (or in some editions *No One Left to Lie To: The Triangulations of William Jefferson Clinton*). I've often thought that if Bernie Sanders (or his campaign manager Jeff Weaver) had more of a killer instinct, he might have had his staff buy up *No One Left to Lie To* in bulk and distribute it for free at campaign rallies.

During the 2016 election cycle, Bernie relentlessly advocated a single-payer "Medicare for All" system whereby healthcare would be funded by progressive taxation and made free at the point of service. One of Hillary's main lines of response was to trumpet her own record of fighting for healthcare reform. In March 2016, for example, she said this:

> We are going to pull together and stay together and stand up against these powerful forces. And I always get a chuckle when I hear my opponent talking about it. Well, I don't know where he was when I was trying to get healthcare in '93 and '94, standing up to the insurance companies, standing up to the drug companies.

The response from the Bernie camp was to dispute the premise that Bernie wasn't present and accounted for in 1993-4. In one memorable picture, the Congressman from Vermont is literally standing behind the First Lady at an event on healthcare reform.

But this response just grants what should absolutely not be granted—that Hillary Clinton was "standing up to the insurance companies" and "standing up to the drug companies" in an attempt to "get healthcare" in any sense remotely comparable to what Bernie was proposing in 2016. Bernie was pragmatic enough to support just about *any* reform that might alleviate any of the harms of America's dystopian healthcare system, but that doesn't mean the Clintons wanted what he wanted. Here's Hitch on exactly that point in *No One Left to Lie To*:

> Had the masses risen up against the insurance companies [in response to the Clintons' populist appeal] they would have discovered that the four largest of them—Aetna, Prudential, Met Life, and Signa—had helped finance and design the "managed competition" scheme which the Clintons and their Jackson Hole Group had put forward in the first place. These corporations, and the Clintons, had also decided to exclude from consideration, right from the start, any "single-payer" or "Canadian-style" solution. A group of doctors at

the Harvard Medical School, better known as Physicians for a National Health Program, devised a version of single-payer which combined comprehensive coverage, to include the 40 million uninsured Americans, with free choice in the selection of physicians. The Congressional Budget Office certified this plan as the most cost-effective on offer. Dr David Himmelstein, one of the leaders of the group, met Mrs Clinton in 1993. It became clear, in the course of the conversation, that she wanted two things simultaneously: the insurance giants "on board," and the option of attacking said giants if things went wrong. Dr Himmelstein laid out the advantages of his plan, and pointed out that some 70 percent of the public had shown support for such a scheme. "David," said the First Lady, before wearily dismissing him, "tell me something interesting."

Hitchens goes on to describe the Clintons' plans as embodying "the worst of bureaucracy and the worst of 'free enterprise'" in its "labyrinthine complexity." As any American reader who's unlucky enough to have ever had to navigate her state's healthcare exchange to buy a "bronze-level" insurance plan should instantly recognize, the "Hillarycare" scheme that went nowhere in '93 and '94 wasn't a predecessor to what Bernie was trying to do in 2016. It was an early attempt to do what Barack Obama *succeeded* in doing in 2010.

"Obamacare" was a Rube Goldberg contraption of bureaucratic complexity. Healthcare was still treated as a commodity, but that commodity was supposed to be made more affordable by layers of regulatory engineering. At its heart was the idea that people buying coverage on exchanges would be able to pick and choose between horrifically complex health insurance plans (and punish over-charging providers by switching plans) as easily as customers drive past one gas station to stop at another where gas is ten cents cheaper. That worked out so well that by 2016 a candidate who openly called himself a socialist won twenty-two primaries and caucuses, in the most anti-socialist country in the developed world, by promising to scrap the Obamacare experiment and just nationalize the whole vile industry.

A *successful* Clinton administration initiative was the "welfare reform" bill that Bill Clinton signed into law in 1996. Here's how Hillary Clinton described what she and her husband were doing in a column from March 2000:

> Since we first asked mothers to move from welfare to work, millions of families have made the transition from dependency to dignity.

In her 2003 memoir *Living History*, Hillary brags that she "worked hard to round up votes for its passage." Here's Hitchens in *No One Left to Lie To*, using the example of Tyson Foods—a company that had donated Bill Clinton's various campaigns since the beginning of his career—to illustrate how this "reform" worked in practice:

> Tyson Foods uses the Direct Job Placement scheme as its taxpayer-funded recruiting sergeant. The first shock of recognition, experienced by those who are supposed to be grateful for a dose of nonalienated and dignified labor, is the "puller job." This involves gutting birds—later to provide tasteless nourishment at the tables of the badly off—at a rapid rate. The fingernails of the inexperienced are likely to be the first to go; dissolved in bacteria and chicken fat. Of Missouri's 103,000 poultry workers, according to the Bureau of Labor Statistics, almost one-third endured an injury or an illness in 1995 alone...Supplied by the state with a fearful, docile labor force, the workhouse masters are relatively untroubled by unions, or by any back-talk from the staff. Those who

have been thus "trimmed" from the welfare rolls have often done no more than disappear into a twilight zone of casual employment, uninsured illness, intermittent education for their children, and unsafe or temporary accommodation. Only thus—by their disappearance from society—can they be counted as a "success story" by ambitious governors, and used in order to qualify tightfisted states for "caseload-reduction credits" from the federal government. The women among them, not infrequently pressed for sexual favors as the price of the ticket, can be asked at random about the number of toothbrushes found in the trailer, and are required by law to name the overnight guest or the father of the child if asked. Failure or refusal to name the father can lead to termination of "benefits" or (even better word) "entitlements." We were once told from the bought-and-sold Oval Office itself, that "even presidents are entitled to privacy": it seems now that *only* presidents and their wealthy backers can claim this entitlement.

If Hitchens had beaten cancer in 2011 and lived long enough to write about the 2016 election, it's safe to say that he would have had nothing positive to say about Hillary Clinton's campaign for the Democratic nomination. Would he have supported Bernie Sanders?

I'm honestly not sure. If we assume for the sake of simplicity that Hitch's politics didn't change in any way during those five years, he would have agreed with some of Bernie's positions and strongly disagreed with others.

What we *can* assert with something approaching certainty is that he would have been horrified when Hillary Clinton bragged in one of her debates with Bernie that Henry Kissinger was a trusted friend and adviser. I'm confident that Hitch would have nodded along with at least grudging respect when Bernie responded that he was proud *not* to count Kissinger among his friends. However else his politics would have evolved between 2011 and 2016, it's difficult to imagine a version of Christopher Hitchens who could hear the name "Henry Kissinger" without being filled with visceral disgust.

Anthony Bourdain once said that after you've visited Cambodia, "you'll never stop wanting to beat Henry Kissinger to death with your bare hands." Even if you've never been within a thousand miles of southeast Asia, you can get a bit of that feeling from reading Hitchens's book *The Trial of Henry Kissinger*. Page after page, chapter after chapter, you learn about Kissinger's personal role not just in overseeing a bombing campaign that led to oceans of death and suffering in Cambodia, but in illegally sabotaging peace talks that could have ended the larger war five years earlier on pretty much the same terms Nixon and Kissinger eventually agreed to in Paris, in plotting the overthrow of democratically elected left-wing governments in various 'third-world' nations, and much, much more.

Yet the pudgy man standing in black tie at the Vogue party is not, surely, the man who ordered and sanctioned the destruction of civilian populations, the assassination of inconvenient politicians, the kidnapping and disappearance of soldiers and clerics and journalists who got in his way? Oh, but he is. It's exactly the same man.

The Clinton book (1999) and the Kissinger book (2001) are representative of the kind of work that Hitchens was best known for during the first three decades of his writing career. The very first book with his name on the cover, all the way back in 1971, was a collection of essays by Karl Marx and Fredrich Engels. (Hitch edited it and wrote the introduction.) Between that book and his death in 2011, he wrote hundreds of articles and almost two dozen books about literature and politics and history. His central focus only veered into more abstract philosophical territory in the last decade of that 40-year career.

Hitchens was a convinced Marxist for the great majority of his adult life. There are religious socialists like Cornel West and Terry Eagleton — or for that matter like many of the priests and nuns killed by CIA-backed death squads in Latin America — who have found ways to combine some of Marx's ideas about history and politics and class struggle with a progressive interpretation of Christian theology, but Hitchens was as much of a materialist and an atheist as Marx himself.

In his *Introduction to a Critique of Hegel's Philosophy of Right*, Marx wrote that "the criticism of religion is the prerequisite of all criticism." Religion was an important source of consolation for oppressed people, Marx wrote, but this kind of consolation ultimately does more harm than good by teaching people at the bottom of society to meekly accept their lot in life.

> The abolition of religion as the illusory happiness of the people is the demand for their real happiness. To call on them to give up their illusions about their condition is to call on them to *give up a condition that requires illusions*. The criticism of religion is, therefore, *in embryo, the criticism of that vale of tears* of which religion is the *halo*.
>
> Criticism has plucked the imaginary flowers on the chain not in order that man shall continue to bear that chain without fantasy or consolation, but so that he shall throw off the chain and pluck the living flower.

In the same spirit, in his memoir *Hitch-22*, Hitchens praises the poet Philip Larkin for his "very moving, deliberate refusal of the false consolations of religion." In the same passage, he rattles off a long series of political disagreements with Larkin, whose "pungent loathing for the Left, for immigrants, for striking workers, for foreigners," and so on showed that "you couldn't have everything." That Hitchens even as a young socialist thought that Larkin's atheism counted for *something* in the face of that list suggests something about how seriously he took the issue.

In 1982 Hitchens wrote a review of a book called *The Politics at God's Funeral* by Democratic Socialists of America founder Michael Harrington. Hitchens acknowledged that Harrington had "honestly lost his faith" but faulted the DSA founder for believing that battles between religion and "anticlerical atheism" were no longer relevant in the modern world.

> Whenever Western reactionaries are in a tight corner, they proclaim to be defending "Christian civilization." The child martyrs of the Iranian army, drafted before their teens, are told by their mullahs that an Iraqi bullet will send them to Paradise. The Polish workers were enjoined by their spiritual leaders to spend their spare time on their knees. What sort of advice is that?
>
> The list runs on — anybody who has seen an Israeli election knows that the mere mention of the holy places of Hebron or Jerusalem is enough to still the doubters and divide the dissidents. And everybody knows that the "Christian Democratic" parties of Europe have a reserve strength of religious iconography they deploy when they think nobody is looking. We are not as far out of the medieval woods as some suppose.

You can find Hitchens saying things like this here and there through the 80s and 90s, but it wasn't a major part of his output until the 2000s. It was a surprisingly small element even in his 1995 book, *The Missionary Position: Mother Teresa in Theory and Practice*. Hitch made the case that Mother Teresa was a cruel and bigoted hypocrite, that she squandered donations while the sick and dying men and women in her care suffered unnecessarily, and that she was all too happy to lend her aura of saintliness to murderous right-wing dictators like Haiti's Jean-Claude "Baby Doc" Duvalier. But he wastes very little time on the *theology* of the woman he'd elsewhere called a "thieving fanatical Albanian dwarf."

He criticizes the Catholic Church's positions on issues like homosexuality and birth control, but even there his focus is on Mother Teresa's alignment with the "fundamentalist faction within the Vatican." He describes the challenges that faction faced (and continues to face) from gay Catholics who don't think there's anything sinful about their sexuality, from "the populist challenge of so-called 'liberation theology'" and even from some moderately conservative Catholics who think the Church's stance on abortion is cheapened by bundling it with an absurd condemnation of birth control pills. He clearly regards the positions taken on all these issues by "Mother" and the rest of the "fundamentalist faction" as contemptibly reactionary, but the book isn't really anti-Catholic, never mind generically anti-religious.

The closest *The Missionary Position* veers toward the sort of territory that Hitchens spent so much time in during his last decade is the section where he debunks an alleged "miracle" reported by English journalist Malcom Muggeridge, who claimed that BBC footage taken in the dim interior of Mother Teresa's "House of the Dying" in Calcutta showed the scene bathed in a "particularly beautiful soft light." Since he remembered his cameraman Ken Macmillan claiming that "filming was quite impossible in there," Muggeridge concluded that what they were seeing was mysterious "divine light."

Hitchens quotes Macmillan himself, who recalls that the reason he went ahead with filming despite the bad light was that "we had just taken delivery at the BBC of some new film made by Kodak, which we hadn't had time to test before I left, so I said to [the director], 'We may as well have a go.'" When the go went better than expected, Macmillan attributed this to the glory of Kodak.

...and fair enough. But you don't have to be an atheist or an agnostic to grant that Macmillan was better than Muggeridge at what philosophers of science call Inference to the Best Explanation. (Roughly, if two explanations are each *consistent* with the evidence, you should still believe the one that explains it better—by, for example, being simpler, more elegant, and fitting more cleanly with the rest of what we know about how reality works.) As Hitchens knew perfectly well, the world is full of devout, church-going Catholics whose piety doesn't stop them from rolling their eyes when they read about someone in Texas claiming to have seen the image of the Virgin Mary in a tortilla.

The first place I know of where Hitchens turned his polemical firepower in any kind of more sustained way than a book review not on one particular religious figure (or her more gullible acolytes) but on religious belief *per se* is his book *Letters to a Young Contrarian*. Some critics have suggested that Hitchens's crusade against religion was inspired by his reaction to the September 11 terrorist attacks, and that's not entirely wrong. 9/11 and the wars that followed in its wake certainly influenced the form of that crusade and lent it an added sense of urgency. But *Letters to a Young Contrarian* was published in the fall of 2001. Hitch would have had to sign off on the final copyedits long before the towers fell. And anyone familiar with his 2007 bestseller *god is Not Great: How Religion Poisons Everything* or his many subsequent debates with pious Christians and Muslims and Jews will recognize all his favorite anti-religious arguments in Letters IX and X.

Here's how he starts Letter IX:

You seem to have already guessed, from some remarks I made in passing, that I am not a religious believer. In order to be absolutely honest, I should not leave you with the impression that I am part of the generalized agnosticism of our culture. I am not even an atheist so much as an antitheist; I not only maintain that all religions are versions of the same untruth, but I hold that the influence of churches, and the effect of religious belief, is positively harmful. I do not wish, as some sentimental materialists affect to wish, that they were true. I do not envy believers their faith. I am relieved to think that the whole story is a sinister fairy tale.

To lay my own cards on the table, I agree with almost everything that Christopher Hitchens wrote about politics between 1971 and 2001. (Two of the most important exceptions covered over by that "almost" involve Yugoslavia and the Falkland Islands.) And as a confirmed philosophy nerd who enjoys arguing about subjects like the foundations of morality, the apparent conflict between free will and determinism, and, yes, the existence or non-existence of God, I share Hitchens's basic commitment to atheism. I even find parts of his humanistic moral critique of religion compelling. But I've never been entirely sold on his politicized "antitheism."

Some of the specific things Hitchens would say in his post-2007 polemics against the faithful reflect his post-2001 political shifts. But as we've seen, he was already a committed antitheist in 1982 (and likely long before). We can and should evaluate the merits of his position on religion *a la carte*.

In chiding Harrington for overestimating the extent to which we're "out of the medieval woods," Hitchens correctly captured some of the politically reactionary uses to which religion has been put by forces ranging from Western European "Christian Democrats" to Iranian mullahs. But this leaves open the question of how the Left can or should respond to our enemies' religious appeals. Is focusing on "anticlerical atheism" likely to be the most effective strategy?

An obvious opening move on the other side of this strategic

argument would be to notice the far more positive political uses to which religion has been put by the South American "liberation theologians" mentioned above or by North American figures like Dr Martin Luther King, Jr. and Rabbi Abraham Joshua Heschel, who marched together first for civil rights and then to end the war that, as Christopher Hitchens would put it in *The Trial of Henry Kissinger*, led to tens of thousands of Americans and "an uncalculated number of Vietnamese, Cambodians and Laotians" losing their lives. When the Western reactionaries Hitchens talked about in his critique of Harrington start proclaiming that they're defending "Christian civilization" or religious Zionists do the equivalent to defend atrocities in Palestine, it seems quite likely that left-wing pastors and rabbis are going to be in a better position than intellectual atheists like Christopher Hitchens (or me) to counter these appeals.

Hitchens's response to suggestions like this one in the Harrington review ("Better Off Without") and in a similar essay published in Harpers in 1983 ("The Lord and the Intellectuals") was to suggest that there was something dishonorable or condescending about the attitude of secular materialists who praised the religious Left.

> Most irritating of all, there are still people on the Left who say feebly that, "after all, there are many 'progressive' church people. Look at the Maryknolls or Archbishop Romero." This is usually said by those who are not themselves religious but who feel that religion is good enough for other people— usually other people in the Third World.

That's a good line. But *is* it dishonorable or condescending for people with different views on abstract metaphysical issues to agree to disagree on those issues while happily working together to pursue shared political goals?

My position is the one advocated by my late friend Michael

Brooks in the final chapter of his 2020 book *Against the Web*. Influenced by Amartya Sen and, through Sen, by the political philosopher John Rawls, Michael emphasized that the values that inform the global fight for democracy and socialism can be found in, for example, Islam, not because the essential nature of Islam is politically progressive—Michael denied that vast and historically heterogenous cultural traditions *have* essential natures—but because at least some human beings in every society are likely to find their way to these values (and to find ways to express them in the distinctive language of any particular tradition). All I need to accept a religious believer as a political ally is that (a) they share a basic vision of justice that can be rooted in what Rawls called the "overlapping consensus" of numerous belief systems and (b) they share a commitment to cultural and religious pluralism.

In other words, if you don't want to impose your religious beliefs on me, I have no *political* problem with you and I'm happy to work with you to achieve a better society. Once we've overcome the severe economic inequality generated by the capitalist system, and the poverty, workplace authoritarianism, and grinding financial stress that afflict the human beings caught on the bottom end of that inequality, we'll all have much more leisure time to engage in intrinsically valuable human activities like creating art and music, traveling, experiencing one another's cultures—and, oh yes, arguing about philosophy.

## Chapter Two

# Hitchens and His Evangelical Critics as Philosophers

In one of Plato's most memorable dialogs, Socrates argues with a seer named Euthyphro about the definition of "holiness." The holy, Euthyphro says, is that which the gods love. Socrates asks him if the gods love the holy *because it is holy* or whether it is holy *because the Gods love it*.

A slightly altered form of this "Euthyphro Dilemma" has convinced a great many philosophers, including more than a few thoughtful religious believers, that divine commands by themselves can't explain much of anything about morality. Assume for the sake of argument that the Lord really did instruct Moses to carve "Thou Shalt Not Kill" on a tablet. Is killing wrong *because God prohibited it*, or did He prohibit it *because it's wrong*? If you choose the second horn of the dilemma, you've conceded that something other than God's will makes killing wrong. If you embrace "Divine Command Ethics" by picking the first horn, you have a different problem. What if the text God had dictated for Moses's tablets had been, "Thou shalt kill whosoever from among thy neighbors thou findest annoying and steal their possessions" or "Thou shalt not under any circumstances be kind or charitable or help little old ladies cross the street"? If Moses had come down from Mt Sinai carrying both of these tablets, and he'd accurately written what the Lord had told him to write, would that make theft and neighbor-killing genuinely morally praiseworthy and charity and kindness and helping little old ladies cross the street genuinely morally objectionable?

Note that if what you're thinking is, "Oh, but God never *would* command such horrible things because those things are morally bad and God is morally good," you've just abandoned Divine

Command Ethics and conceded that murder and the rest are morally wrong for some reason other than God's disapproval of them.

A wide range of other reasons have been offered over the course of the subsequent twenty-four centuries of moral philosophy—and especially during the spurt of philosophical productivity that characterized the last four. So, for example, virtue theory, most associated with Plato's student Aristotle, holds that the morality or immorality of our actions can be located "upstream" of the actions themselves in the character traits that cause us to act that way in the first place, while utilitarians like John Stuart Mill locate it "downstream" in the good or bad consequences of those actions.

I owe this handy visual metaphor to my graduate school professor Michael Slote, who liked to illustrate it with arrows on a chalkboard. To see how these two conceptual options lead to different moral conclusions, think about two versions of the Trolley Problem.

The first comes from Philippa Foot (in her essay "Abortion and the Doctrine of Double Effect"):

Edward is the driver of a trolley whose brakes have just failed. On the track ahead of him are five people; the banks are so steep that they are not able to get off the track in time. The track has a spur leading off to the right, and Edward can turn the trolley onto it. Unfortunately, there is one person on the right-hand track. Edward can turn the trolley, killing the one; or he can refrain from turning the trolley, killing the five.

The second comes from Judith Jarvis Thomson, who named the problem in her classic essay "The Trolley Problem":

George is on a footbridge over the trolley tracks. He knows

trolleys and he can see that the one approaching the bridge is out of control. On the track back of the bridge there are five people; the banks are so steep that they will not be able to get off the track in time. George knows that the only way to stop an out-of-control trolley is to drop a very heavy weight into its path. But the only available, sufficiently heavy weight is a fat man, also watching the trolley from the footbridge. George can shove the fat man onto the track in the path of the trolley, or he can refrain from doing this, letting the five die.

As Thomson points out, most people have a utilitarian reaction to Foot's original example. The consequence of turning the trolley is better than the consequence of refraining, so turning is the right thing to do. But most of us have a very *un*-utilitarian reaction to Thomson's version of the case. Pushing the man has a better consequence than refraining, but it still seems to be very obviously the *wrong* thing to do. When I've presented these cases to classrooms of twenty-five students, I've had at least twenty raise their hands for "who here thinks the right thing to do is to turn the trolley?" and no more than one or two for "who here thinks the right thing to do is push the man?" And it's hard not to wonder about the one or two.

A virtue ethicist might be able to explain why our intuitive revulsion at the prospect of George pushing the man is morally relevant—even though the "downstream" consequences of turning the trolley or refraining are identical to those of pushing the man or refraining. Someone with a well-developed sense of compassion likely wouldn't be able to bring themselves to push another human being onto a trolley track, and according to the virtue theorist this "upstream" fact is enough to explain the immorality of George killing the man.

Slote's visual metaphor breaks down in the case of Kantians, who believe that the morality or immorality of an action is innate in the nature of the action itself. It's never permissible to reduce a person to the status of a "mere means to an end." (The "mere" is important. If I ask a friend to help me move a couch, I'm using him as a means to an end. If I push him onto a trolley track, I'm treating him "merely" as a means to an end.) Immanuel Kant believed that, while we only deserve moral credit for following this "Categorical Imperative" if we're motivated by respect for the moral law for its own sake, violating it is *always* wrong.

Kant's views on subjects like the proper relationship between masters and servants weren't even slightly progressive, but socialist thinkers ranging from Eduard Bernstein to Cornel West have run with his fundamental insight and drawn anti-capitalist conclusions. (If a large class of the population is kept desperate enough to be willing to accept positions not as worker-owners of democratically managed cooperatives but submissive wage laborers taking orders for eight hours a day and handing over a large share of what they produce to the boss in the form of profits, it can be argued that decisions by business-owners and politicians that preserve the economic status quo amount to treating humans of that class as "merely a means" to capitalist ends.) Other philosophers like Robert Nozick started with quasi-Kantian premises and drew starkly different political conclusions.

Moral philosophy is complicated and difficult. The three historically important theories I've sketched out are very far from exhausting the possibilities and there's plenty of room for people who are thinking hard about these issues to disagree. Crucially, though, one thing *every* thinker I've just name-checked agrees on—even the ones who were themselves believing Christians—is that postulating the existence of a God who tells you to act in a certain way does nothing to explain *why* acting in that way is morally desirable. The argument derived from Plato suffices to show that if God exists and is in the business of issuing commands, either those commands are arbitrary (in which case, while it might be in your self-interest to follow them so you aren't punished, they don't have any *moral* force) or God is commanding you to act in this way because it's morally desirable for some other reason than that He commanded it. And that "some other reason" is going to be equally available to theists, atheists, and agnostics.

Some Divine Command Ethicists think they can get around this problem by saying that God's commands aren't arbitrary because they flow from His unchanging moral character, but this just pushes the question back by one step. Assume for the sake of argument that God's nature is steady, compassionate, and loving. If instead it had been capricious, cruel, and hateful, would *that* have counted as a "morally good" character? If not, God's actual character must be good for some other reason than that it's *God's* character. And this evaluation too is going to take place on grounds equally available to nonbelievers.

At this point in the argument, some Divine Command Ethicists will insist that moral goodness is definitionally a characteristic of God, so the all-powerful but morally wicked being under consideration wouldn't count. That's fine, but it won't help them get out of the Euthyphro problem. If the wicked but all-powerful being in this thought experiment would have been a being other than God rather than a wicked version of God *because* the being's moral character was wicked, then we need a reason to call that character wicked other than it not being "God's" character...and we're right back where we started.

Something like a Euthyphro-based argument might be what Hitchens was getting at when he'd throw down his favorite challenge during his frequent post-*god is Not Great* debates with religious believers. "Let someone name one ethical statement made, or one ethical action performed, by a believer that could not have been uttered or done by a nonbeliever."

That always struck me as a slightly unhelpful way to frame the point for at least two reasons. We can get at the first one by asking whether performing an exorcism, for example, counts as a "moral action." It certainly is if demons are real and exorcism works! Similarly, a fundamentalist who believes that converting his agnostic friends to Christianity will save them from eternal torment also has at least some reason to think that sharing the gospel with his friends is a moral act.

In other words, if all Hitch's interlocutors were being asked to do was to name something a believer would (but a nonbeliever wouldn't) say or do that would count as moral *on the assumption that the believer's religious beliefs are true,* that challenge is pretty easy to answer—even if we don't cheat by counting a belief in Divine Command Ethics as one of the religious beliefs we're assuming for the sake of argument. On the other hand, if the challenge was to name a statement a believer could make or an action a believer could (and that a nonbeliever at least *wouldn't*) perform that would count as moral even if every single one of the believer's religious beliefs were false, it doesn't seem to me that Hitch's point has much force.

Take an apparently common combination of beliefs on the contemporary religious Right. Like Rene Descartes, many such Christians seem to believe that the mostly hairless mammal you see when you look at a mirror is not "you." The "you" doing the thinking, feeling, remembering, planning, and so on isn't even your physical brain. You're an immaterial and immortal soul that currently happens to be closely associated with your body—so much so, Descartes says, that as a matter of day-to-day practicality, the two form a single unit—but which will continue to exist and continue to think and feel even after your body dies. This isn't always what Christians believed. Medieval thinkers tended to have a different and more obscure view about bodies, souls, and the resurrection of the dead that were inspired by a Christian reading of Aristotle. But the simple Cartesian picture, combined with the belief that God somehow gives fertilized eggs souls right at the moment of conception, seems to be the default conceptual picture for most contemporary Christians who think that abortion is murder.

It's worth noting that it would be possible to accept these premises and resist the conclusion that ensouled fetuses have a right to life that overrides a pregnant woman's right to control her own body. As Hume reminds us, we can only ever get from premises about facts to conclusions about values with the help of premises about values. Even so, there's no point denying that accepting the religious anti-abortionist's factual premises at least takes us a long way in the direction of accepting their preferred moral conclusion. Given all of that, if Hitchens challenges a religious anti-abortionist to name a moral action they would perform but that an atheist would not and the religious anti-abortionist responded, "work to end the killing of the unborn," should they be impressed by the response that *by the atheist's lights* abortion isn't wrong? Or should they say that the fact that atheism typically blinds people to the important moral truth that abortion is wrong is a strike against atheism? By analogy, if I meet a white nationalist who tells me she believes that black and brown people are too irrational to be capable of self-government, the fact that her moral and political conclusions *would* be less repugnant *if her factual starting points weren't nonsense* wouldn't much interest me in the absence of the slightest reason to take those starting points seriously.

Of course, I don't think the two situations are epistemically or morally comparable. I think the religious anti-abortionist is wrong on all counts. (Hitchens, oddly, could be a bit squishy and ambivalent about this topic.) I believe that abortion rights are important, that a day-old zygote doesn't count in any morally important sense as a "person," that the right to life has to be weighed against the right to bodily autonomy even when we're talking about very late fetuses with a more plausible claim on personhood, and that Cartesian dualism is an absurd and indefensible theory of the mind. (While we're at it, I also don't think there's a God.) But I can't see how any of these arguments are advanced by asking what action or statement *that a secular materialist would regard as being morally good* would be done or said by a theist but not by an atheist.

So that's the first problem. As one of Hitchens's regular sparring partners, Pastor Douglas Wilson, might have put it, to even understand the "name one ethical statement made, or one ethical action performed" challenge we need to pick a "presupposition" about the truth of various morally relevant religious beliefs. And depending on which one we pick, the challenge is either an easy one for believers to meet or one that they have little reason to lose any sleep over.

The second problem with this formulation is that if we take Hitch's "could" literally, the challenge is both trivially unanswerable and entirely unimportant. Any believer or nonbeliever *could* make any moral statement or perform any moral action. If "could" means "could do so without being philosophically inconsistent," the Euthyphro Argument against Divine Command Ethics is decisive. If, on the other hand, the real question is whether a nonbeliever *would* make any moral statement or perform any moral action that a nonbeliever *would* say or do, things get more complicated.

Another of Hitchens's evangelical friends and sparring partners, Larry Taunton, says that Hitch himself acknowledged that some of his most religious friends *were* willing to do admirable things in their personal lives that he couldn't really imagine himself doing. Christopher's brother, Peter Hitchens, was and is a pious member of the Church of England. (He's also so politically conservative that Christopher once said that he felt the need to wear a "garlic necklace" to get through Peter's book *The Broken Compass*.) In his book *The Faith of Christopher Hitchens: The Restless Soul of the World's Most Notorious Atheist*, Taunton quotes a disarmingly honest assessment that Christopher made of their respective characters.

I was asked by someone what the difference in personality was, and found myself replying that if my wife and I were both to die I was sure Peter would offer to look after my children. I had not known I was going to say this, and I leave the second half of the thought uncomfortably un-uttered.

Similarly, Taunton reports that Hitchens was deeply surprised to learn that Taunton and his wife, who already had three children, had adopted an HIV-positive Ukrainian girl named Sasha. Taunton reports Hitchens saying, "I am glad there are people like you in the world, I really am, but I cannot for the life of me understand why you would do it."

Taunton seizes on the second half of that sentence as evidence that, as an atheist, Christopher must have been literally *incapable of understanding* why the Tauntons adopted Sasha.

Had any Christian friend of mine said such a thing, I would have been disappointed. A Christian would know why Lauri and I (or anyone else) would want to adopt an orphan: because our Lord commands us to care for those whom he called "the least of these." The point isn't that every Christian must or should adopt. It is, rather, that every Christian must or should know *why* we would do so. If, however, you are an atheist, where exactly is the moral imperative? If this world is all that there is, why not milk this life for all that you, and you alone, can get out of it? Christopher knew very well that there was no compelling reason not to do precisely that.

This is, I have to say, pretty weak tea. For one thing, if Taunton really believed that Hitchens was only interested in milking this life for all that he and he alone could get out of it, he would have to be very confused about the political causes to which his friend devoted the great bulk of his life—not to mention the moral fervor that Hitchens so clearly brought to their debates about religion. Does he really believe that his friend was a moral nihilist?

For another, Taunton himself clearly doesn't believe that he had a moral *obligation* to adopt Sasha. ("The point isn't that every Christian must or should adopt.") He believes that it's the kind of action that philosophers call supererogatory— morally praiseworthy but not morally obligatory, or in simpler language "above and beyond the call of duty." And the first half of Hitchens's statement makes it clear that he thinks the same thing. ("I'm glad that there are people like you in the world, I really am.") If he didn't understand the reason why this was a good thing to do, why would he be glad there are people in the world who did it?

Putting aside Taunton's slightly unsavory attempt to milk a lesson in the connection between Godlessness and immorality from an overly literal interpretation of his dead friend's casual turn of phrase, the clear meaning in context of "I cannot for the life of me understand why you would do it" is "I cannot for the life of me understand *how* you *could* do it." In other words, Hitchens understood at least some of the limitations of his own moral character and he was willing to honestly acknowledge those limits and praise people like his brother or Larry Taunton for doing things he regarded as objectively morally admirable but which he didn't personally believe he would be able to bring himself to do.

Similarly, my friend Eli—who, I should add, is as much of an atheist as I am—donated a kidney without having a specific recipient in mind. Due to her academic interests, she'd read a lot of bioethics papers about kidney donations and spent a lot of time thinking about the issue and she was morally moved to give up one of her own kidneys to save someone she didn't know. I can't imagine doing that. I don't feel particularly guilty about not doing it, since I don't think anyone has an *obligation* to part with a piece of their body, but I do admire her for doing it.

On the other hand, if we interpret Hitchens's challenge as being to name a moral statement or action that at least *some* believers are likely to say or do (even if most won't), and that *fewer* nonbelievers would say or do, Taunton might have a point. It's possible that, if your moral feelings are mixed up with mental states typically associated with intense religiosity—feelings like awe and wonder and a sense of transcendence—then as a matter not of logical entailment but psychological fact you end up being somewhat more likely to work up the motivation to engage in moral heroism, both in interpersonal contexts like adopting Ukrainian orphans and in some political contexts (like risking your life to help slaves escape from bondage in the antebellum South). Intense religiosity might not be the *only* factor that can nudge people in such directions—my guess is that Eli isn't alone and that academics with an interest in bioethics are generally somewhat more likely to donate kidneys than the general population, for example—but it's certainly an important and widespread factor, and one that at least complicates Hitchens's moral case for antitheism.

His response to this would presumably be the one hinted at in the second challenge he'd routinely issue to anyone who thought that believers had a moral advantage over nonbelievers. "Can you think of an evil statement made, or a wicked action performed, precisely because of religious faith?"

The implied answer to this second question is the one made explicit in Hitchens's writings on the subject, which are full of examples ranging from medieval Christian persecutions of Jews to the horrors committed by Orthodox Jewish settlers against Palestinians on the West Bank to the Taliban shooting little girls in the head for going to school, as well as relatively mundane examples like culturally mainstream parents and pastors in advanced countries routinely psychologically scarring young children by teaching them to worry that they'll burn for all eternity when they die. If he was right to suggest that (a) all of these things are primarily a result of religious belief *per se* and (b) they collectively outweigh both the routine acts of kindness and charity and the rare but striking acts of moral heroism that religion can inspire, he has at least the beginnings of a good moral case that atheists should also be antitheists—in other words, that rather than just seeing theism vs. atheism as an innately interesting philosophical issue, worth pursuing out of a sense of intellectual curiosity, atheists have a moral imperative to try to "deconvert" the faithful.

Evaluating the truth of (b) is difficult as an empirical matter. Perhaps for every good-hearted Christian who adopts an HIV-positive child from a distant country, there's one who kicks his son out of the house or sends him to gruesome "conversion therapy" for being gay (or who adopts a Ukrainian orphan but treats her the way the mom in Stephen King's *Carrie* treated *her* daughter), but I don't know where we'd begin to get the data that we'd need to make that kind of determination. Let's accept at least for the sake of argument that Hitchens is right to think that the harms of religion outweigh the social benefits. Let's even grant the part of his historical case against theism that feels most like a stretch—his insistence in *god is Not Great* and elsewhere that the crimes of atheistic dictators are an indirect part of the damage done by religion, since for example without the Orthodox Church training Russians to accept the Tsar as a representative of God's will, thus building up habits of credulity and obedience, Stalin wouldn't have been able to convince so many Soviet citizens to accept his despotic rule. (Counterpoint: Many millions of Russians somehow overcame this training when they overthrew the old order in 1917.)

That would still leave us with a lot of open questions about (a). All too often Hitchens talks, for example, about the role played by the "parties of God" in various twentieth and twenty-first century conflict zones in terms that almost make it sound like, rather than being motivated by mundane geopolitical considerations and using religion to *rationalize* their crimes, these parties really had been *caused by an otherworldly power* to start shooting and bombing each other.

Imagine that Christianity had, like various other minor Jewish heresies before it, faded away long before the birth of the Emperor Constantine. The Roman Empire would never have been Christianized and Christianity wouldn't have been the religion of both the aristocracy and the peasantry of feudal Europe. The Crusades and the Inquisition certainly wouldn't have happened. But would whatever happened instead have been *better*?

Hitchens himself dips a toe in the water of this kind of speculation in *god is Not Great*. He brings up the trove of ancient non-canonical gospels found at the Nag Hammadi site in Egypt. In one, the "Gospel of Judas," Jesus is revealed not to have been the son of the God of the Old Testament but as an "avatar of Seth, the third and little-known son of Adam." At the Passover dinner, Jesus reveals that he came to Earth from Barbelo, a "motherland beyond the stars," and that he "is the one who will show the Sethians the way home." As part of this plan, he awards Judas the "special mission of helping him shed his fleshly form and thus return heavenward."

Deranged science fiction though this is, it makes infinitely more sense than the everlasting curse placed on Judas for doing what somebody had to do, in this otherwise pedantically arranged chronicle of a death foretold. It also makes infinitely more sense than blaming the Jews for all eternity. For a long time, there was incandescent debate over which of the "Gospels" should be regarded as divinely inspired. Some argued for these and some for others, and many a life was horribly lost on the proposition. Nobody dared say that they were all man-inscribed long after the supposed drama was over, and the "Revelation" of Saint

John seems to have squeezed into the canon because of its author's (rather ordinary) name. But as Jorge Luis Borges put it, had the Alexandrian Gnostics won the day, some later Dante would have drawn us a hypnotically beautiful word-picture of the wonders of "Barbelo." This concept I might choose to call "the Borges shale": the verve and imagination needed to visualize a cross section of evolutionary branches and bushes, with the extraordinary but real possibility that a different stem or line (or tune or poem) had predominated in the labyrinth. Great ceilings and steeples and hymns, he might have added, would have consecrated it, and skilled torturers would have worked for days on those who doubted the truth of Barbelo: beginning with the fingernails and working their way ingeniously toward the testicles, the vagina, the eyes, and the viscera. Non-belief in Barbelo would, correspondingly, have been an unfailing sign that one had no morals at all.

So far none of this poses any sort of problem for Hitchens's case against religious belief. In *god is Not Great*, he talks about the damage done not just by Christianity but by Islam, Judaism, and even (as a very brief afterthought) Buddhism and Hinduism. If the aristocracy and peasantry of feudal Europe had believed in Sethianism/Judaism instead of (what we would recognize as) Christianity, things would have been just as bad — and *that's his point*. "Religion" in general poisons everything.

But the point about Barbelo can be extended in a way that endangers Hitchens's case, especially when we remember that — even in the final decade of his life when his relationship to socialist politics got a lot more ambiguous — Hitchens continued to profess that he found Marxism compelling as a theory of *history*. As late as a 2004 exchange with Norman Finkelstein, we find Hitchens praising Marx's theory as "a method of examining the dynamics of the economy and society, now adopted because of its relative rigor by a number of non-Marxist historians," and recommending G.A. Cohen's excellent book on the subject. Finkelstein had faulted Hitchens for inconsistency, saying that on one page Hitch "claims to be persuaded by the 'materialist conception of history,' but in the next sentence he states that 'a theory that seems to explain everything is just as good at explaining nothing.'" Hitchens's response was that if you say that there's a contradiction between these two claims, you're defaming the Marxist theory of history. Marx's actual theory, Hitchens says, wasn't rigid and deterministic. Fair enough. The problem, though, is that even the loosest, most nuanced, and least deterministic version of the "materialist conception of history" would still be...well...materialist. In other words, in explaining historical events it would emphasize what Marxists call material *forces* and *relations*—roughly, the level of economic development and the way any given economic system is organized—rather than seeing the subjective ideas in people's heads as the primary drivers of history.

To see the problem for Hichens' combination of views, take the Borges/Hitchens thought experiment about the Gospel of Judas several steps further. Imagine that *all belief in gods* had somehow gone extinct during the late Roman period. (To answer your question, no, I can't imagine a set of circumstances that would have led to this actually happening. Humor me anyway.) This would have meant that the justifying ideology of European feudalism couldn't have been Christianity or anything like it. But would it have been anything like the enlightened and pluralistic secular humanism beloved by Christopher Hitchens?

In a series of back-and-forth essays with the aforementioned neo-Calvinist theologian Douglas Wilson anthologized as *Is Christianity Good for the World?*, Wilson raises the specter of Stalinist Russia as an example of atheist immorality. In my own debate with Wilson, I pointed out that the Nordic countries have some of the highest rates of non-belief on the planet but (a) none of them seem to be run by a Stalin or a Pol Pot and (b) they all seem to have far lower rates of interpersonal violence than, for example, the United States. If there are enough other differences between the cases that this isn't a laboratory experiment on the moral effects of atheism, it at least seems to show that the combination of Godlessness and an expansive welfare state doesn't lead to a mass outbreak of citizens deciding that, since there is no God, everything is permitted. Instead of bringing in this kind of empirical evidence, Hitchens's tack in *Is Christianity Good for the World?* is to argue that the Stalinists were the wrong *kind* of atheist. "If Mr Wilson," he wrote, "would prefer to compare like with like and point to a society that lapsed into misery and despotism by following the precepts of Epicurus or Spinoza or Jefferson or Einstein, I will gladly meet him on that ground."

Notice that with the exception of Epicurus, who considerably predated the rise of feudalism, all of these figures were produced by the modern world. If you accept the "materialist theory of history," here's how you explain that: the development of what Marxists call the "productive forces" of society made the continued existence of feudalism a hindrance to further economic development.

Crudely boiling centuries of complicated and messy historical development down to a skeletal description, instead of a traditional agricultural society needing peasants bound to aristocrats' estates by a complicated network of feudal rights and duties, an emerging industrial society needed cities full of people who possessed what Marx acidly called a "double" freedom. That means they were legally free to make employment contracts with any capitalist who came along, and they were also "free" from any means of supporting themselves *except* selling 8 hours a day (or, during the early period of capitalism, 16 hours a day) to an employer.

The rise of liberal democracy facilitated this process. This and the extreme importance to the new society of rapidly developing scientific knowledge created an intellectual environment where Spinoza, for example, didn't die in obscurity after being excommunicated from Amsterdam's rigidly orthodox Jewish enclave for heresy. He found many friends and admirers outside those communal walls and he was able to keep writing under the protection of a reasonably friendly legal regime.

Marx thought the relatively enlightened democratic liberalism that's played such an important role as a justifying ideology of capitalism stops at a relatively shallow understanding of freedom. He believed that the most important kind of freedom was *freedom from domination*, and argued that the development of the productive forces of a society by capitalism creates the possibility that the working-class majority could take over that society and run it in their own interests—collectively owning the factories, for example, and electing their own managers, and crucially also democratically deciding among themselves how to divide up the fruits of their labor between various socially beneficial uses.

Much of Christopher Hitchens's life was dedicated to pursuing a twentieth-century version of this political project. Martin Amis recalls that when he and Hitchens worked together at *The New Statesman*, they'd exchange "taunts and teases" about Hitch's socialist commitments. The far more moderate Amis would accuse Hitchens of wanting to be ruled over by ordinary unsophisticated workers Amis called "yobs" and "berks." "You want to be ruled by yobs," he would tell him. "Not just rule in their interests and in their name—but rule *by* yobs." Hitchens embraced the charge. "I live for the day when the berks are finally in the saddle."

Putting these future possibilities to one side, though, the point is that if the justifying ideology of feudalism had been something other than Christianity, it certainly wouldn't have been "the precepts of Epicurus or Spinoza or Jefferson or

Einstein." Feudal society could only function with strong ideological medicine to keep their vastly more savagely ground-down version of "berks" in their place—and whatever alternative medicine they came up with, it's plausible that it would have led to its own laundry list of atrocities.

Wilson himself doesn't make any of these points in response to Hitchens. Far from being a historical materialist, he's the pastor of a right-wing megachurch who dabbles in apologetics for the Confederacy. (In the debate with me, he casually referred to economic redistribution of even the moderate welfare-state variety as "statist thievery.") Instead, Wilson argues that even if atheists don't *happen* to behave badly, they don't have any good *reason* to refrain from doing so.

[T]he point is not whether we could rustle up some nice places governed by atheists or some hellholes governed by Christians. If given a choice between living in a Virginia governed by Jefferson and living in a Russia under the czars, I would opt to live under your beloved Jefferson. Fine. But this is not a concession, because it is not the point.

Take the vilest atheist you have ever heard of. Imagine yourself sitting at his bedside before he passes away. He says, following Sinatra, "I did it my way." And then he adds, chuckling, "Got away with it, too." In our thought experiment, the one rule is that you must say something to him, and whatever you say, it must flow directly from your shared atheism—and it must challenge the morality of his choices. What can you possibly say? He did get away with it. There is a great deal of injustice behind him, which he perpetrated, and no justice in front of him...I am certainly willing to take the same thought experiment. I can imagine some pretty vile Christians, and if I couldn't, I am sure you could help me. The difference between us is that I have a reason for condemning evil in its Christian guise. You have no basis for confronting evil in its atheist guise, or in its Christian guise, either.

However many Christians are monsters and however many atheists live like saints, Wilson insists, Christians have an advantage because atheists have no "rational basis for rational condemnation" of wrongdoing by either believers or nonbelievers. Elsewhere in the exchange, he takes up one of Hitchens's favorite examples—the genocide that God commands the Israelites to perpetrate in the Old Testament—to make the same point.

> Picturing an Israelite during the conquest of Canaan, doing every bad thing that you say was occurring back then. During one of his outrages, sword above his head, should he have stopped for a moment to reflect on the possibility that you might be right? "You know, in about three and a half millennia, the consensus among historians will be that I am being bad right now. But if there is no God, this disapproval will certainly not disturb my oblivion. On with the rapine and slaughter!"

"On *your* principles," he taunts Hitchens, "why *should* he care?"

Taken seriously, this is a remarkable admission. Wilson is confessing to not being able to understand the distinction between self-interested motivations and moral ones. (If you would be horrified by someone who told you the only thing that stopped them from committing rape or murder was the possibility of arrest and imprisonment, then congratulations— you *do* understand that distinction.) Taunton makes the same confession when he says that "if this world is all there is" you might as well "milk this life for all that you, and you alone, can get out of it."

Tweak Wilson's example about the Canaanite. Let's stipulate

that the all-powerful creator of the universe *had* commanded the Israelites to treat the people of Canaan the way Bosnian Serb militias treated Muslims in Srebrenica. Notice that I say, "the all-powerful creator of the universe," not "God." As noted above, some theists insist that a morally depraved entity can't count as "God" as they use that term. Fine. Assume for the sake of argument that the universe was created and is ruled not by a benevolent God but by an all-powerful demon.

While we're at it, assume that the Israelite warrior Wilson imagines, the one with his sword raised mid-air as he contemplates his options, knows the creator's will in this matter for a certainty and knows with equal certainty that his demonic creator will punish him if he declines to participate in "the rapine and the slaughter." If he hesitates, he does so out of compassion for his Canaanite victim. Which version of that warrior is *morally* better—the one who refuses to participate even knowing that he's endangering his immortal soul, or the one who swallows his doubts and does as he's told?

There may be good reasons to reject Hitchensian antitheism, but those good reasons aren't to be found anywhere within ten thousand miles of *here*. The nicest thing you can say about Wilson and Taunton is that they're out of their depth. This gets even clearer in Taunton's case when he switches from misinterpreting stray remarks to prove that his dead friend was incapable of understanding morality because he didn't believe in God to misinterpreting other such remarks to prove that Hitch was teetering on the edge of a religious conversion.

Taunton reports that Hitchens described Sam Harris's version of utilitarianism as a "weak and untenable philosophy" and that he expressed various disagreements with the great utilitarian moral philosopher Peter Singer. He presents these comments as signs that Hitchens's "reflexive atheism was showing significant cracks in it" rather than simply that Hitchens disagreed with one of several competing secular visions of morality. He also can't quite seem to make up his mind about where the cracks are located. Does atheism entail moral nihilism ("why not milk this life for all that you, and you alone, can get out of it?") or does it entail utilitarianism—a demanding moral doctrine that often requires self-sacrifice for the greater good?

He also takes Hitchens befriending some of the evangelicals he debated and staying up late happily talking to them about their beliefs as evidence that, as he puts it in one entirely italicized sentence, "*Christopher Hitchens was a searcher.*" He talks about Hitchens's late-in-life political shifts and suggests that he was in the middle of a similar shift on metaphysical issues.

> Up to this time in his life, Christopher understood Christianity to be either a relic of the past that was only alive through its ceremonial role in the culture (Anglicanism) or a religion that oppressed Third-World peoples through "myth and mystery," as Dostoevsky's "Grand Inquisitor" put it (Catholicism). But his debate tours brought him into contact with Christians of a different type, people who spoke of a relationship with Jesus Christ. Rather than the knuckle-scraping, fundamentalist hell-sending caricatures he expected, he found many evangelicals to be intelligent, thoughtful, compassionate, and perhaps most surprising, he found himself enjoying the company of many of them. And so, once again, his enemies had become his friends.

Squinted at in just the right light, this can be made to sound like the start of a trajectory that might have led him to privately accept Jesus at death's door. The problem is that these religious "debate tours" started with the book tour for *god is Not Great* and in that very book Hitchens makes it clear that none of this was out of character for him.

I trust that if you met me, you would not necessarily know

that this was my view. I have probably sat up later, and longer, with religious friends than with any other kind. These friends often irritate me by saying that I am a "seeker," which I am not, or not in the way they think.

If Taunton ever read this book, it certainly wasn't fresh in his memory when he wrote *The Faith of Christopher Hitchens*. Taunton cites a line in *Hitch-22* where Hitchens whimsically talks about the possibility of a "Protestant atheism" and calls this a "sign of thawing" that the post-*god is Not Great* debate tours had brought about in Hitch's attitude toward Christianity. But here's what Hitchens wrote in *god is Not Great*:

I now know enough about all religions to know that I would always be an infidel at all times and in all places, but my particular atheism is a Protestant atheism. It is with the splendid liturgy of the King James Bible and the Cranmer prayer book—liturgy that the fatuous Church of England has cheaply discarded—that I first disagreed.

In a quote for a February 2021 article in *The New York Times*, Hitchens's literary agent Steve Wasserman insinuated that Taunton was lying about the "unverifiable conversations" Taunton says he had with Hitchens. I'm inclined to disagree. Nothing that Taunton says Hitchens said to him sounds particularly implausible to me. It's his *interpretation* of those conversations that's absurd.

For example, Taunton quotes Hitchens as saying, in a discussion about a passage in the Gospel of John about death and resurrection, "I'll admit that it is not without appeal to a dying man." I can believe that he said that. Hell, I can damn near *hear* him saying it in my head. But the way that Taunton insists on treating this as an indication that Hitchens was sliding in the direction of faith actually manages the trick of making me feel embarrassed on behalf of a nasty little fundamentalist like Larry Taunton. Hitchens had made the exact same point—that belief in an afterlife would be emotionally desirable, and that it was a bit sad that his atheism deprived him of this form of comfort—almost a decade before he met Larry Taunton, in the pages of *Letters to a Young Contrarian*.

> I do not delight in the thought of my annihilation, and I am not always consoled even by David Hume's stoic reflection that, after all, I was also nothing before I was born.

And this single sentence—"I'll admit that it is not without appeal to a dying man"—is by far the *best* conversational evidence that Taunton produces anywhere in the book. He puts it two paragraphs from the end of the last chapter.

A more typical bit of "evidence" comes a hundred pages earlier when Taunton reports a conversation between himself, Hitchens, and Professor John Lennox about the Eastern Orthodox Churches. Hitchens had mentioned atrocities committed by those churches in a debate earlier that night. Lennox and Taunton challenged him on the basis that any Christians who would act that way weren't *real* Christians and that therefore none of these atrocities counted against the record of *real* Christianity. Hitchens, Taunton claims, was "astonished" and "dumbfounded" and lapsed into silence to "process" this response.

That's how Taunton interprets *every* lapse into silence recounted in the book. It never seems to occur to him that sometimes people lapse into silence because they've lost interest in the conversation or they have already said everything they have to say or they just got an idea for a new article for *Vanity Fair* or they're preoccupied with worry about their rapidly spreading esophageal cancer. Speaking for myself, at least, I can even think of a time or two in my life when a friend said something truly asinine and I decided to let it go.

## Chapter Three

# Drink-Sodden Former Trotskyist Popinjay?

In 2005, British MP George Galloway called Christopher Hitchens a "drink-sodden former Trotskyist popinjay." The two men would later have a public debate at Baruch College in New York, but nothing either of them said there was as memorable as the original insult.

There was certainly some truth to the "drink-sodden" part. A few years later, when an interviewer asked Hitchens (a) what things he couldn't be without when he traveled, and (b) what his favorite whiskey was, Hitch responded that those sounded like the same question to him. (The single answer was Johnny Walker Black.) In his introduction to Martin Amis's father Kingsley's book *Everyday Drinking*, Hitchens considers and rejects the maxim that alcohol is "a good servant but a bad master." This is a "nice try," he says, but the "plain fact" is that it "makes other people, and life itself, a good deal less boring."

In a 2003 piece in *Vanity Fair*, Hitchens recommended observing "the same rule about gin martinis—and indeed all gin drinks—that you would about female breasts: one is far too few and three is one too many." Responding to this in *CounterPunch*, Hitchens's former colleague at *The Nation* magazine, Alexander Cockburn, said he'd seen the man have trouble bringing "a lighted match and the first cigarette of the morning into productive contact." Cockburn concluded that Hitch was "more of a six-breast guy."

By 2010, Hitchens had probably heard more than enough of this kind of thing to start feeling defensive. In a *Slate* article called "A Short Footnote About the Grape and the Grain," he protests at the fantastical stories being told about his nights of boozing. Houseguests and interviewers, he says, were constantly bringing him bottles of Johnny Walker, as if they were propitiating a "demon."

He doesn't exactly want them to stop but he does want to set the record straight. He points out his industrious schedule of speaking, writing ("at least a thousand words of printable copy every day"), classroom teaching, and debates. Could he really do all this if he were a hopeless drunk?

> I work at home, where there is indeed a bar-room, and can suit myself. But I don't. At about half past midday, a decent slug of Mr Walker's amber restorative, cut with Perrier water (an ideal delivery system) and *no ice*. At luncheon, perhaps half a bottle of red wine: not always more but never less. Then back to the desk, and ready to repeat the treatment at the evening meal. No "after dinner drinks" — most especially nothing sweet and never, ever any brandy. "Nightcaps" depend on how well the day went, but always the mixture as before.

How about the rest of Galloway's charges? If, like me, you'd never heard anyone say "popinjay" in any other context, it's an archaic word for parrot and an only slightly less archaic word for a vain and pompous person. (Think "peacocking.") As with the question of whether the schedule of daily drinking described in "On the Grape and the Grain" sounds like a little or a lot, I'll leave the fairness or unfairness of the "popinjay" charge to the judgment of the reader.

The part about Hitch's earlier affinity for the politics of assassinated communist dissident Leon Trotsky, on the other hand, is unambiguously true—even if reasonable people can disagree with Galloway's insinuation that this is a bad thing.

To understand what "Trotskyism" even is, we have to start with a quick tour of the factional splits in the early socialist movement. In most contexts, Marx and Engels used the terms "socialism" and "communism" interchangeably to talk about the radically democratic alternative they hoped would supplant capitalism after a wave of revolutions did away with the kings, tsars, and kaisers who ruled continental Europe. In advanced capitalist democracies like the US and the UK, they were cautiously optimistic that the working class could take power through the electoral victories of socialist parties—although even there they worried that factory-owners would react to this development the way plantation-owners had reacted to the election of Abraham Lincoln.

They spent very little time outlining what socialism/communism would actually look like, although there are hints scattered around their voluminous writings. They regarded the ultra-democratic Paris Commune of 1871 as a model of what the post-revolutionary transition to such a society would look like and mentioned the few worker-owned cooperative businesses that already existed under capitalism as important harbingers of this future society, since they demonstrated in practice that "modern industrial production" was possible without dividing society into "a class of masters" and a subordinate "class of hands."

This much is easy enough to follow. As unpredictable as the ripple effects of such a dramatic change in the fundamentals of the economic and political order would be in practice, it's not hard to imagine at least the broad outlines of what a modern economy would be like if it wasn't divided into workers and "capitalists" (business-owners) because every firm was either democratically operated by the workers themselves or was directly controlled by a democratic state (perhaps in combination with some level of worker-autonomy on the shop floor). Or at least it's not hard to imagine such a thing if we also imagine that such a set-up continues to share at least some features with the kind of economies that exist all around the world right now—like, crucially, continuing to use markets to coordinate production with consumer preferences so when the emancipated workers of this society went to the grocery story as consumers, the products they wanted to buy would be waiting for them on the shelves.

In various writings, though—notably the *Critique of the Gotha Program*—Marx and Engels strongly suggest that markets would be swept into the dustbin of history at the same time as the division of society into workers and capitalists. In the first chapter of the *Critique*, Marx predicts that workers in a post-capitalist economy would do away with the exchange of money for commodities entirely in favor of a system where non-circulating "certificates" would be issued entitling their bearers to one-time acquisitions of consumer goods proportional to the "duration or intensity" of their labor. Decisions about *what* to produce would presumably be made by some sort of democratically elected planning boards. Marx hopefully added that as technology continued to progress, increased abundance would make these certificates redundant. Everyone could just take what they needed. Meanwhile, as Marx suggests in the "Fragment on Machines" from his *Grundrisse*, less and less of the work necessary to keep an industrial society going would have to be done by people. The resulting job losses would be a nightmare under capitalism, where the alternatives for most of the population are work or destitution, but if automation galloped forward *while the machines were collectively owned*, the result could be that everyone maintained their current standard of living even as less and less work was spread more and more thinly among the entire working population until, Marx suggested, whatever work still had to be done by humans could get done as a side effect of everyone pursuing whatever projects happened to interest them. To translate what I take to be the core of Marx's point here into more contemporary terms, given this level of future technological development and everyone having all the free time they could ever ask for, some people might devote themselves to writing poetry or studying Roman history or just sitting on the couch playing videogames—but enough would devote themselves to computer engineering that the computers themselves could do the rest.

To put my own cards on the table, I think some version of Marx's final-stage idea, now sometimes called "Fully Automated Luxury Communism," is an inspiring ideal worth striving for, even if I regard it as an open empirical question whether humanity will ever get all the way there. I'm far less sold on the bit about labor certificates, and strongly suspect that, if we want to get past capitalism without experiencing the kind of dysfunction that plagued the Soviet economy, any socialist society that would be logistically realistic in the near to medium term would have to incorporate at least some market mechanisms—even if the firms operating within those markets were worker-owned and some crucial sectors of the economy were taken out of the market entirely.

Defenders of capitalism sometimes insist on treating "the market" as a single thing as if there were no important differences between *labor* markets and markets in consumer goods but equating the two makes very little sense in human terms. If you have to sell a precious family heirloom to make ends meet, that's sad. If you have to sell your car and walk everywhere because you can't take the bus, that can make your life more difficult and frustrating. But having to sell half your waking hours to a dictator is just a categorically different thing.

At any rate, in the decades after Marx died, his successors didn't spend much time thinking about these details. Important "social democratic" thinkers like Eduard Bernstein, Karl Kautsky, Rosa Luxemburg, and Vladimir Lenin were too busy arguing about *how* to defeat the capitalist elite and extend democracy to the "social" realm (i.e. the economy) to devote themselves to figuring out exactly how the future society they wanted would work. The prevailing attitude seems to have been that the answers to these questions would be worked out by the victorious working class as historical events unfolded.

This prediction was put to the test in 1917, when the Bolshevik faction of the Russian Social Democratic Party actually did seize power. The Bolsheviks had to not only figure out how to organize a new economy in a hurry but how to do so under horrifically unfavorable circumstances. The revolution had been fueled by the discontent of workers and peasants who'd spent years sending their sons to die for the profits of the rich in what was then called "the Great War," and the Bolsheviks were only able to make peace with the Germans by signing a humiliating treaty handing over huge swaths of territory. Meanwhile, a new war started as domestic counter-revolutionary armies were aided by the military intervention of fourteen nations, including the United States and Britain.

The Bolsheviks won, but they did so at an enormous cost—in resources, in lives, and to the radically democratic ideals for which the revolution was fought in the first place. They were a party of workers and intellectuals concentrated in the cities, but the great majority of the population lived in the countryside. As workers had been electing councils ("soviets") and collectively taking over the cities in 1917, the peasants had been busy dividing up the big estates owned by aristocrats into individual plots of land. Over the course of the years of the civil war, more and more of the workers who'd originally made the revolution fought and died in the Red Army and were replaced by new arrivals from the countryside. Meanwhile, more and more civil liberties and democratic rights were curtailed behind the front as a series of increasingly draconian emergency measures became permanent. The cumulative effect was to create a society that looked less and less like a "workers' state" and more and more like the rule of a caste of state officials over an increasingly disempowered working class and a great mass of often resentful peasants.

In some ways the end of the Civil War actually exacerbated these trends. Here's how Leon Trotsky described the situation in his book *The Revolution Betrayed*:

> The demobilization of the Red Army of five million played no small role in the formation of the bureaucracy. The victorious commanders assumed leading posts in the local Soviets, in economy, in education, and they persistently introduced everywhere that regime which had ensured success in the Civil War. Thus on all sides the masses were pushed away gradually from actual participation in the leadership of the country.

Meanwhile, the socialist movement in the West had splintered into supporters of the Russian Revolution, who now called themselves Communists, and more moderate socialist parties that still used the Social Democratic label. Over the course of the next several decades, these Social Democratic Parties became steadily focused on practical short-term reforms and less invested in the hope of completely transforming society, and "social democracy" became a term for doses of socialism administered within the capitalist system rather than for the kind of workers' democracy that might come *after* capitalism.

When Lenin, Trotsky, Stalin, and the rest of the Bolshevik leadership had originally started the revolution, they'd been confident that it would spread to the far more industrially developed countries of Western Europe. When this didn't happen, a faction fight started within what was now called the Communist Party of the Soviet Union. The Left Opposition led by Trotsky wanted to restore some measure of workers' democracy and believed that the only hope for creating a more advanced version of socialism in the USSR lay through renewed efforts at a world revolution. The dominant faction led by Stalin wanted to focus on building "socialism in one country."

After defeating the Trotskyists (and other opposition factions) and sending the holdouts into exile in Siberia, Stalin put that slogan into practice in a grotesque way. The peasants were herded into "collective farms" that many experienced as a kind of second serfdom while "five-year plans" focused on rapid industrialization at enormous human cost. Workers not only lost the last lingering shreds of democratic self-management in factories but were forced to meet increasingly demanding quotas and shipped to the gulag if they skipped too many days of work.

As the British Trotskyist theoretician Tony Cliff noted in his 1948 book *The Nature of Stalinist Russia,* all of this looked more than a little like a historic echo of the birth of British capitalism "in the sixteenth and seventeenth centuries through the eviction of the peasantry from the land" so that former peasants would have no realistic choice except to go to work under horrific conditions in the early factories that William Blake had called "dark satanic mills." The difference was that this process was far more violent in Russia because it was compressed into a tiny amount of time. "Stalin accomplished in a few hundred days," Cliff wrote, "what Britain took a few hundred years to do."

Different factions of the Trotskyist movement around the world analyzed what was going on in slightly different ways but Cliff's analysis—a more extreme critique of the Soviet system than Trotsky's own, it should be noted—was that the Soviet Union had reverted to capitalism, albeit a mutant form of capitalism in which the state bureaucracy collectively played the role of the old private capitalists. Even so, he thought, workers were exploited just as they were in conventional capitalist firms. In neither system did workers get to decide who their bosses would be or how the value created by their labor would be divided up. The slogan of Cliff's branch of the Trotskyist movement (the International Socialists) was, "Neither Washington nor Moscow but international socialism."

And it was Cliff's International Socialists to which a young Christopher Hitchens was recruited one night in Oxford in 1966. He'd already been a member of the Labour Party, which back then still formally regarded itself as a socialist party committed to "secure for the workers by hand or by brain the full fruits of their industry and the most equitable distribution thereof that might be possible on the basis of the common ownership of the means of production, distribution, and exchange, and the best obtainable system of popular administration and control of each industry or service." (So read Clause IV of the party's constitution until the Clinton-like centrist Tony Blair succeeded in doing away with it in 1995.) Even in 1966, though, Labour was an extremely moderate social democratic party, periodically trading power with the Conservative Party ("the Tories") without British capitalists worrying too much about losing their wealth and property in the process. When Labour governments were in power they made very little effort to turn Clause IV into reality, preferring to administer doses of socialism like universal healthcare and publicly owned coal mines within the basic structure of British capitalism. They were also far too chummy with the American Empire for the tastes of the party's left wing.

Hitchens was already on that left wing, and already a regular participant in demonstrations against the Vietnam War, when he met the International Socialists' Peter Sedgwick for a drink. "If a pint of tepid British beer can be said to have acted as a catalyst," Hitchens later wrote, "then this encounter changed my life."

Before reading the IS pamphlets Sedgwick gave him that night, Hitchens had already read and been impressed by some of the writings of Karl Marx—but, he remembers in *Hitch-22*, he had questions.

Had not the postwar social changes in Britain rendered the

idea of "class" somewhat obsolete? Were the trade unions not a self-serving interest bloc? And wasn't the failure of Communism in Russia and Eastern Europe a demonstration of the failure (to put it no higher) of the Communist idea? Only in countries like apartheid South Africa, whose goods I was already boycotting, could anything so dogmatic have a residual appeal. These were among my objections to moving any further to the left than I already had.

Sedgwick put these reservations to rest, introducing young Hitchens to both the militant shop-floor movement in British workplaces that was shaking up the sleepy status quo of the trade union movement and those Eastern European dissident movements who dreamed not of turning back the clock from "state capitalism" to regular private capitalism but of advancing to socialist democracy. *Neither Washington nor Moscow but international socialism.*

Five years later, we find Hitchens writing an introduction to a collection of essays by Marx and Engels about the previously mentioned Paris Commune—a brief but momentous event in 1871 in which ordinary French workers and soldiers took advantage of the chaos caused by the end of the Franco-Prussian War to seize control of the city government of Paris. They instituted a series of dramatic reforms ranging from making every state official recallable by their constituents at any time and for any reason (and capping their salaries at the average wage of a skilled worker) to turning over factories abandoned by fleeing owners to be run democratically by associations of workers, all of which so terrified the ruling classes all over Europe that there was a joint Franco-Prussian effort to crush this experiment in working-class self-rule.

In his introduction to the 1971 volume, Hitch is careful not to present the Commune as a neat-and-tidy socialist fairy tale. He considers complicating facts and divergent interpretations from non-Marxist historians, conceding a point here or there, but he still concludes that nothing these historians bring up constitutes a serious challenge "to the core of Marx's case" — that the Commune represented "a new form of politics resting on the energies of the mass of people." Indeed, he writes, many of Marx's later critics "recognize precisely this, albeit often with the symptoms of alarm with which conservatives habitually regard such discoveries."

The Commune was a major inspiration for the labor and socialist movements in the final decades of the nineteenth and the first decades of the twentieth century. Lenin danced in the snow on the day when his new Soviet Republic officially outlasted the two months and ten days of the Paris Commune. But in 1971, Hitchens saw the authoritarian system shaped by Lenin's heirs as part of the problem to be solved by the efforts of those dissidents, East and West, who continued to be inspired by the "ideals of the Commune." He wrote:

It does not seem to me that the Europe of 1971 is in any position to be complacent about the ideals of the Commune, either from the point of view of what is desirable or of what is practical. A continent has been divided into two blocs; both increasingly centralized economically, both geared to war production as a central factor of prosperity, both locked into an upward spiral of international competition which subordinates all human needs to the priority of growth and accumulation, and both conducting this business, while armed with weapons of total destruction, at the expense of those two-thirds of humanity who are condemned to the poverty, hunger, and disease known as "under-development."

Three decades later, in the context of an unusually sharp disagreement with one of his oldest friends, we still see Hitchens insisting on a clear distinction between the original ideals of the

Paris Commune (and the Russian Revolution) and the system that had existed in the "Eastern bloc" countries in the twentieth century. The debate started with Martin Amis's 2002 book *Koba the Dread*. The main subject was Stalin (the "Koba" of the title), but Amis's book grew out of his horror at his ex-Trotskyist friend failing to feel appropriately repentant about his past politics. Amis seems to take it as an axiom that all versions of communism are the same in every important way. Thus, if Hitchens started out as a Trotskyist and even in 2002 didn't fully disavow that part of his political history, he *might as well* have been an unrepentant Stalinist. Moreover, Amis believes, Stalinism (and hence Trotskyism) is as bad as fascism. Having worked through the premises of this little syllogism, Amis startles himself with the conclusion that his old friend *might as well* be an unrepentant fascist.

I should pause here to note that Martin Amis is a very good novelist. He's also written many interesting literary essays. Any reader familiar with this body of work might be reluctant to believe that the man could be quite this much of a simpleton about history and politics. Surely, I'm caricaturing his argument.

Hold that thought while you read Amis's description of a debate between Christopher and Peter Hitchens about the European Union. (Christopher wanted to Remain and Peter wanted to Leave.) The debate took place at Conway Hall in London.

[T]he audience was passionately interactive: fierce questions posed in fierce regional accents, drunken braying by "name" journalists, and, from various rotund politicos, the occasionally resonant "hear hear"…which sounded like "erdle erdle" which made you think of an enormous stomach digesting an enormous meal. At one point, reminiscing, Christopher said that he knew this building well, having spent many an evening in it with many an "old comrade." The audience responded as Christopher knew it would (the remark was delivered with a practiced air): the audience responded with affectionate laughter.

Afterward, I asked [anti-Communist historian Robert] Conquest, "Did *you* laugh?"

"*Yes*," he said.

And I said, "And so did I."

Why is it? Why is it? If Christopher had referred to many meetings with many "an old blackshirt," the audience would have...Well, with such an affiliation in his past, Christopher would not be Christopher...Is that the distinction between the little moustache [Hitler] and the big moustache [Stalin], between Satan and Beelzebub? One elicits spontaneous fury, and the other elicits spontaneous laughter?

Amis's horror at the laughter at Conway Hall that evening ultimately led to the book whose full title was *Koba the Dread: Laughter and the Twenty Million*. In the subsequent exchange of articles and open letters, Hitchens makes a heroic attempt to explain to his friend that (a) not all varieties of far-left thought are identical to each other, (b) the differences between them have been hugely historically important, and (c) equating "Communism" with fascism is politically illiterate and morally obscene. He also points out that, in claiming that no one laughed at Hitler, Amis seems to have forgotten about Charlie Chaplin — who incidentally *really was* a pro-Soviet "fellow traveler" (but whom no one with a functioning moral compass would call the equivalent of a Nazi).

In his *Atlantic* essay "Lightness at Midnight" (a play on the title of Arthur Koestler's classic anti-Stalinist novel *Darkness at Noon*), Hitchens invites Amis to think a bit harder about the relevant history. Before the successful Russian Revolution in 1917, there had been a "dress rehearsal" revolution in 1905, complete with soviets of workers deputies and prominent roles being played by some of the same figures who would lead the Bolsheviks to power twelve years later. It's plausible that, had the revolution succeeded the first time, without Russian society being ravaged in the meantime by far more than its fair share of the destructive effects of World War I, things would have played out very differently. The brutality on all sides of Russia's postrevolutionary civil war happened against a background where the value of human life had already been severely cheapened.

The best-case scenario would have been that the revolution spread to the West, toppling the Kaiser and preventing World War I (and hence World War II) from happening in the first place. It would have helped that the socialist movement throughout Europe wouldn't have been badly fractured by the traumatic experience of socialist parties in most of the belligerent nations surrendering to mass patriotic hysteria, each supporting "their own" ruling class in the war. Of course, there's no guarantee that this is what would have happened—but it takes an extreme degree of dogmatic anti-communism to just help yourself to the assumption that a victory by rebellious workers and peasants at any time in Russian history would have necessarily led to the exact same end point of gulags and forced collectivization.

Even many readers who are much less sympathetic than Hitchens was to the tradition of anti-Stalinist Marxism might nod along here. And this alone takes us to an important disanalogy between communism and fascism. It's doubtful that anyone anywhere imagines that, if only the Beer Hall Putsch had succeeded and Hitler had come to power ten years earlier, the result would have been any more humane and democratic than the version of the Third Reich that existed in our timeline.

Granted, the Beer Hall Putsch took place after World War I as well. The rise of the Nazis is itself a striking piece of evidence in support of Hitchens's point about the widespread collapse of the value of human life throughout war-ravaged Europe. But it's also impossible to imagine a Hitler-like demagogue building a successful street-fighting mass movement and coming to power in Germany *in 1905*. A country that hadn't gone through that level of trauma would never have been vulnerable to Nazi takeover in the first place.

Hitchens writes:

> Excuse me, but nobody can be bothered to argue much about whether fascism might have turned out better, given more propitious circumstances. And there were no dissidents in the Nazi Party, risking their lives on the proposition that the Führer had betrayed the true essence of National Socialism. As Amis half recognizes, in his *en passant* compliment to me, the question just doesn't come up.

In 1968, the Communist Party of Czechoslovakia embarked on a series of reforms to try to create what liberalizing communist leader Alexander Dubček called "socialism with a human face." This experiment, popularly known as the Prague Spring, was crushed by Soviet tanks. When Amis was a first-year student at Oxford, he attended a small protest against the intervention. In *Koba the Dread*, he contrasts the "sorrowful" and "decent" atmosphere he remembers from that rally to the wild "emoting and self-lacerating" of the giant crowd at a protest against the Vietnam War at the American embassy in Grosvenor Square. The lesson is the same one Amis drew from the unseemly laughter at Conway Hall—that Western liberals and leftists don't take communist crimes as seriously as anti-communist ones.

As he continues his summary of the unrest around the world that year, Amis includes, for example, a stray line about "barricades in Paris." This is a reference to the combination of a student uprising at universities and a general strike by French workers that came shockingly close to toppling the government of Charles de Gaulle. Amis's point is to paint a picture of the New Left that emerged in this era as basically unserious ("revolution as play") and far too naïve about the dangers of communism.

In an open letter to Amis published at *Slate*, Hitchens makes several related points. First, Amis wasn't at the Grosvenor Square protest, but he was. Were Hitchens and other protestors emoting? No kidding. Hundreds of thousands of Vietnamese peasants were being shot, blown up, or literally having their skin burned off with napalm as they screamed in agony. The My Lai massacre had happened literally the day before the demonstration. News hadn't yet emerged of that particular horror but the protestors at Grosvenor Square had a pretty good idea of the general picture.

As to the Soviet suppression of the Prague Spring, far from Hitchens and his comrades treating it as an afterthought, the International Socialists "organized pro-Czech events around the country and even managed to fling leaflets in Russian on to the decks of Soviet merchant vessels in British ports." Hitchens himself was in Cuba, where he'd been attending an internationalist youth conference, on the day of the invasion, and he recalls that he managed to distribute some Trotskyist literature in Havana. (In *Hitch-22*, he notes that while Fidel Castro was unwilling to condemn the Soviet invasion for obvious reasons, popular opinion in Cuba seems to have very much been on the side of the Czech reformers—he recalls that during the crisis anyone who looked Russian was "greeted with little showers of pebbles and dogshit and the taunt 'Sovietico'" in the streets of Havana.) Where Amis brings up Czechoslovakia to portray the New Left of 1968 as indifferent to the crimes of Stalinism, Hitchens makes the point that the Establishment in both East and West was being threatened by the same wave of global rebellion.

The regimes themselves seemed to get the point. Moscow

directly ordered the French Communist party to help put down the rebellion against De Gaulle, and Brezhnev both sought and received Lyndon Johnson's advance assurance that a Red Army invasion of Prague would be considered an "internal affair."

It's bad enough that Amis seems to feel that the purity of his anti-Stalinism would be compromised if he acknowledged the existence of any important political conflicts between different groups that could be broadly described as "communist." But equating all sides in such conflicts with *Nazis* is grotesque.

[Y]our attempted syllogism invites a direct comparison with Hitlerism, and levels the suggestion of moral equivalence to the Nazis at, say, the many "hard left" types who worked for Dr Martin Luther King. My provisional critique of this ahistorical reasoning would fit into three short italicised sentences. *Don't. Be. Silly.*

This is very good. It's also more than a little jarring to read it in an open letter published by Christopher Hitchens in *September 2002*. At that time, he was very far from being the "Comrade Hitchens" he had been in the 1970s—or even in the 1980s when he wrote this passage for *The Nation*:

In the charmed circle of neoliberal and neoconservative journalism..."unpredictability" is the special emblem and certificate of self-congratulation. To be able to bray that "as a liberal, I say bomb the shit out of them," is to have achieved that eye-catching, versatile marketability that is so beloved of editors and talk-show hosts. As a lifelong socialist, I say don't let's bomb the shit out of them. See what I mean? It lacks the sex appeal, somehow. Predictable as hell.

*This* Hitchens is (to a very great extent) the same one who wrote *No One Left to Lie To* at the end of the 1990s. Crucial pages of that book are devoted to Bill Clinton's decision to bomb the El Shifa pharmaceutical plant in Sudan, which Clinton alleged to have been financed by Osama Bin Laden as part of a scheme to manufacture nerve gas. A great many observers suspected that the Clinton administration's main objective in latching onto this claim and bombing the plant was to get a news cycle that wasn't dominated by Monica Lewinsky. In any case, a night watchman was killed in the bombing itself, and the loss of the main source of medicine and pesticide in the country led to tens of thousands more deaths in the coming years.

Hitchens painstakingly debunks the government's many lies about the bombing. The evidence of a link to Bin Laden was always dubious, and the administration had so little confidence in its own claim about nerve gas that it moved to block UN inspectors from investigating the rubble. The actual owner of the plant, one Saleh Idris, was able to finance a private investigation and to use the results to demand financial compensation.

At the time he wrote *No One Left to Lie To*, Hitchens thought Idris would succeed. He didn't—his lawsuit was rejected not because his case was weak (it wasn't) but on the basis of the argument that the bombing was a "political question" not best handled by the courts. Despite the misguided optimism on behalf of Idris, Hitchens's comment on all of this is interesting as a window into his politics at the end of the 90s.

As a capitalist and holder of private property, Mr Idris was always likely to receive due consideration if he was prepared to hire the sorts of help that are understood in the Clintonoid world of soft money and discreet law firms. The worker killed at the plant, the workers whose livelihood depended upon it, and those further down the stream whose analgesics and antibiotics never arrived, and whose names are not recorded, will not be present when the recompenses are agreed. They were expendable objects of Clinton's ruthless vanity.

Similar sentiments are found in *Why Orwell Matters*, which was published in 2002 but seems to have been written sometime before September 11, 2001. Hitchens effusively praises the semi-Trotskyist Spanish politician Andres Nin in that book. He compares Nixon and Kissinger going to China with the constant shifts in alliances between authoritarian states in Orwell's *1984*. "Oceania has *always* been at war with Eurasia..."

The September 2002 version of Hitchens is noticeably further than he'd been when he wrote these books from being the Trotskyist he'd been in the 70s or even the somewhat more moderate radical—still a socialist, and still with quite a bit of residual Trotskyism in his political bloodstream—that he'd been for decades after that. He eviscerated Amis's "attempted syllogism" about socialism and fascism *not* because he was still a socialist but because he was still too intellectually honest to let that kind of ahistorical drivel stand.

As is true of many people who undergo political conversions and deconversions, Hitchens's shift seemed abrupt at the time but in retrospect it reflected changes in his perspective that had been developing for a long time. The Iraq chapter in *No One Left to Lie To*, for example, is much less likely to resonate with any Bernie-loving, *Jacobin* magazine-reading contemporary leftist reader than the rest of the book. Rather than being outraged about Clinton's bombings and sanctions against that country in the way that he's outraged by the bombing of the El Shifa plant, Hitchens—who'd already spent quite a bit of time with Kurdish leaders in northern Iraq—mostly seemed to be upset that the administration was letting Saddam Hussein off too easy. And Hitchens already had a history of occasionally dropping his usual anti-war stance in contexts like the (very brief) British war in the Falklands in the early 80s and the American intervention in the former Yugoslavia in the 90s in which it seemed to him that the American Empire (or its British vassal) was taking sides *against* the sort of quasi-fascist thugs that the empire usually ended up supporting in places like Nicaragua and El Salvador.

Overall, though, the Hitchens who wrote *No One Left to Lie To* and *Why Orwell Matters* and even the fascinating transitional fossil in his political evolution that is *Letters to a Young Contrarian* was one who was more loyal than not to the political ideals that he'd fought for in the 70s. *Neither Washington nor Moscow but international socialism.* The Hitchens that had emerged by September 2002 had explicitly abandoned the possibility of international socialism. In the open letter to Amis he dismisses the idea that "the specter of Trotskyism" could once again "stalk the land" in any sort of serious way.

I am in a strong position to tell you that all such talk is idle. It's over.

He'd already come to that conclusion (though in a more tentative way) in Letter XIV of *Letters to a Young Contrarian*. He continued to recognize a long list of historically important Marxists ("Antonio Gramsci, Karl Liebknecht, Jean Jaures, Dimitri Tucovic, James Connolly, Eugene Debs and others") as "moral and intellectual" giants who deserved great credit for the stand they took against some very real injustices. "For most of my life," he wrote, "I considered myself a modest combatant" in the socialist "cause," but recently "I've been compelled to recognize that its day is quite possibly done." He made it clear that he still had many objections to the reigning system of "monopoly capitalism," but he didn't see much hope of replacing it with anything but a better and presumably less monopolistic version of capitalism. That said, as large as these concessions to his ideological enemies were, his position in Letter XIV represented a *very* incomplete break from his earlier politics. Five paragraphs after the line just quoted, we find him talking like this:

> When I was young, I was consumed by the opposition to the Vietnam War and still wish that I could claim to have done more to help the movement against it. In my university generation there were many young Americans who agonized about the military draft; I was involved in assisting their resistance and I know for a fact that it is completely slanderous to say that they worried chiefly about the wholeness of their own skins. (Well, almost completely slanderous; one of the young Americans of my cohort was the self-seeking dodger Bill Clinton.) The point about the draft, as it seemed to many, was that it was theoretically universal and thus anyone who avoided or evaded it was in effect condemning someone else to go instead. This consideration operated very powerfully on those who were more fortunately placed, since their opposition to the war was of a piece with their support for the Civil Rights movement and the "War on Poverty." ...I thought then and I think now that those who resisted, whether by burning their draft cards or going to jail or going into exile, were absolutely right. There is an obligation, if your "own" government is engaged in an unjust and deceitful war, to oppose it and to obstruct it and to take the side of the victims.

These words read like an indictment of the positions that Hitchens was taking in September 2002. The United States had already invaded Afghanistan and it was gearing up to invade Iraq.

As I write these words, the Biden administration is finally bringing what I and many others called a "forever war" in Afghanistan to a close after *twenty years* of sustained imperial violence—twenty years of American soldiers kicking in doors and terrorizing civilians, of Afghan drivers being killed at roadside checkpoints set up around their country by occupying forces, of Afghan children growing up without parents and Afghan parents burying their children because the military occupying a deeply hostile population was too oblivious to local customs and too hair-trigger in its use of deadly force to tell the difference between a gun being fired by an insurgent and one being fired as part of a wedding celebration.

The invasion was originally justified by the Taliban's failure to hand over Osama Bin Laden, but Bin Laden was eventually killed in un-invaded Pakistan. Once it was clear that the war wouldn't lead to Bin Laden's capture, the goal posts were moved to a noble narrative about spreading democracy and liberating the women of Afghanistan. "Democracy" co-existed about as well with a war of occupation in Afghanistan as it had in South Vietnam, and the friendly regime propped up by American troops fell to the Taliban pretty much the nanosecond that Biden started to pull out troops. (If you believe that another year or for that matter another twenty years of American occupation would have led to a different outcome, I have a whole series of bridges to sell you.) Hitchens had claimed in an article for *The Guardian* in November 2001 that "[t]he Taliban will soon be history." Twenty years later, that quote requires no further commentary.

Meanwhile, the invasion of Iraq being prepared in 2002 was an "unjust and deceitful war" if ever there was one. Bush and his enablers justified that intervention by (a) claiming that Saddam Hussein had "Weapons of Mass Destruction," and (b) claiming to be worried that at some point in the future he might use them himself or share them with Al Queda. Just in case any of this still needs to be said two decades later, the evidence for (a) turned out to be a hodgepodge of half-truths, outright lies, and nonsense whispered into the ears of neoconservatives by Iraqi emigres like Ahmad Chalabi who wanted the Americans to hand them the keys to their country—or whimpered into the ears of CIA torturers by naked and humiliated prisoners desperate to say whatever their captors seemed to want to hear. And (b) never made sense in the first place. Why would a secular tyrant like Saddam Hussein share *any* weapons with his deadly enemies? (Hussein was more than willing to use lurid religious appeals to whip up popular support at crucial junctures, so in that sense he wasn't "secular," but he was very "secular" in that he oversaw a country where women weren't required to wear veils and the kind of Islamist subversives who wanted to change that were brutalized by the secret police. In Hitchens's writings about Iraq, he often fails to make this basic distinction.) Moreover, the idea that if war planners in Country A are worried that Country B *might* attack A at some point in the future, this justifies A in bombing, invading and occupying B—you know, *just in case*—would, if taken seriously, license all sides of every long-simmering regional conflict on the planet to launch all-out wars against each other. It's hard to imagine what the world would look like after a few years of *that*.

That this hasn't happened just shows that everyone understands that empires are allowed to play by different rules to ordinary nations. But if we narrow our focus to Iraq and its neighbors, it's difficult to overstate the amount of horror directly and indirectly caused by the war. The initial assault (dubbed "shock and awe" by the war planners) involved the use of cluster bombs in densely packed neighborhoods of Baghdad and other Iraqi cities, each of which spread explosive material over an area the size of a football field. And that was just how *it* started. Infrastructure destroyed in the bombardment was all too often left in tatters, and when many Iraqis inevitably joined insurgent factions to try to drive out the invaders, American and British forces spent years stomping around the country like a giant monster crushing skyscrapers under its paws. A study in a prestigious medical journal (*The Lancet*) showed that once deaths from fighting were added to deaths resulting from the general chaos, breakdowns in access to electricity and sanitation, and so on, there had already been 654,965 "excess deaths" — that is to say, 654,965 dead Iraqis who would have been alive if George W. Bush hadn't ordered the invasion—by 2006. And this leaves out the mutilations. It leaves out the vast number of human beings displaced from the country as refugees. It also leaves out the indirect destabilizing effects around the region that resulted in, for example, the rise of ISIS.

Not only did Christopher Hitchens not "oppose" and "obstruct" the wars in Afghanistan and Iraq and take the side of the victims, by September 2002 he was already an outspoken defender of the invasion of Afghanistan and advocate of a second invasion in Iraq. He'd somehow gone from *neither Washington nor Moscow but international socialism* to being an ardent supporter of Washington's wars in the Middle East.

As we enter the third decade of the twenty-first century, it should be clear that Hitchens's support for those wars was a moral and political catastrophe. Those of his fans least capable of admitting that he could get something this important this badly wrong will deny it anyway, but anyone still parroting his positions on the "global war on terror" today can be safely dismissed as the neoconservative equivalent of the kind of leftist who could never quite bring himself to admit that Comrade Stalin could have actually done all the things revealed in Khrushchev's speech.

The interesting question is not, *Was Hitch right about Afghanistan and Iraq?* Even those on the Left—and I count myself as one of them—who continue to admire the man's overall body of work need to acknowledge that the answer to *that* question is a giant NO written in fire. Whatever value there may be in certain aspects of what he had to say about religion or literature or half a dozen other subjects during his final decade, and however worthy of renewed interest his earlier work may be (not least his earlier work on the subject of American imperialism), Late

Hitchens's positions on what Westerners bloodlessly refer to as "foreign policy" were indefensible.

The question that's still worth asking as we trace his evolution over the course of his long career as a journalist, essayist, and debater isn't about the merits of where he ended up. It's *How the hell could he have ended up there?*

## Chapter Four

# Hitchens in Nine Debates

You can see it happen, a little at a time, if you watch enough hours of Hitch doing his thing. The record is all over YouTube. These nine confrontations, on issues ranging from socialism and capitalism to the record of the Catholic Church to the existence of God to whether Britain should leave the EU, show you where he started, where he ended up, and some of the threads that started to unravel along the way.

I.    Hitchens and Said vs. Lewis and Wieseltier: "The Scholars, the Media, and the Middle East" (1986)

The debate starts with a strange presentation by Bernard Lewis. He says people have been talking up this event as a gladiatorial contest or a bullfight or as the "shootout at the MESA Corral." (The venue is a meeting of the Middle East Studies Association.) He assures us that he's only interested in polite scholarly discussion.

He makes some general comments about how scholars in every field feel that the media ignorantly misrepresents their area of expertise. He handwaves a bit about how Islam both is and isn't like other religions. People often say that the Koran is the Muslim Bible and Friday is the Muslim Sabbath and none of that is exactly wrong but he thinks the differences are profound enough that such comparisons obscure more than they clarify. And anyway, we'd all agree that it would be absurd to say that the Torah was "the Jewish Koran" or that the Gospel was "the Christian Koran," wouldn't we? So there you go.

Oh, and all cultures stereotype one another. Muslim travelers to the West will speak of "loose women" just as Western travelers to the Middle East will speak of "licentious men." He jokes that, had these stereotypes been accurate, it would be a bit of a mystery why the two groups "didn't get on better."

At this point, and for most of the rest of the presentation, it's hopelessly unclear what thesis is under consideration. It's even less clear what Lewis has to say about it. He's swaggering and making jokes—but when you zoom out a little and think about what he's doing, it looks like he's nervously avoiding the nub of the issue.

Finally, when he has one minute left, he turns to...pie.

What I shall offer are general principles of how I feel a scholar ought to behave. You will probably say, "Yes, that's apple pie." To which I would answer, "Maybe." But don't forget, we are living in a time when apple pie is under attack, when we are told that since perfect apple pie is impossible, we should eat raw dough and crab apples. I don't share that opinion.

The "general principles" he goes on to articulate are platitudes about civility and a "decent level of debate" and the like. But he never quite says how this "apple pie" is under attack or who's attacking it or how any of this has to do with the advertised subject.

Things get clearer when the second speaker, Edward Said, comes to the podium, not only because he's far better at getting to the point but because *he's the one* that Lewis is accusing of telling everyone to eat raw dough and crab apples. The "shootout at the MESA corral" is happening in the first place because of the controversies rocking Middle East Studies due to the increasing popularity of Edward Said and his ideas about Western "Orientalism" — roughly the essentialist Western discourse about Mysterious and Exotic Easterners (with a particular focus on Arabs and Muslims).

Said's book with that title, published in 1978, focused on the sins of "the scholars." He took on "the media" in 1981's *Covering Islam*. In his presentation, he reverses that order. Where Lewis just finished vaguely mumbling about how all scholars grumble about the way their particular expertise is handled by the media, Said is brutally specific, listing six major themes that characterize Western coverage of the Middle East.

One. The pervasive presence of generally Middle Eastern, more particularly Arab and/or Islamic, terrorism, Arab or Islamic terrorist states and groups, as well as a "terrorist network" comprising Arab and Islamic groups and states backed by the Soviet Union, Cuba, and Nicaragua. "Terrorism" here is most often characterized as congenital, not as having any foundation in grievances, prior violence, or continuing conflicts.

Two. The rise of Islamic and Muslim fundamentalism, usually but not always Shi'i, associated with such names as Khomeini, Qadhdhafi, Hizballah, as well as, to coin a phrase, "the return of Islam."

Three. The Middle East as a place whose violent and incomprehensible events are routinely referred back to a distant past full of "ancient" tribal, religious, or ethnic hatreds.

Four. The Middle East as a contested site in which "our" side is represented by the civilized and democratic West, the United States, and Israel. Sometimes Turkey is included here, most often not.

Five. The Middle East as the locale for the re-emergence of a virulent quasi-European (i.e. Nazi) type of anti-Semitism.

Six. The Middle East as the fons et origo, the hatching ground, of the gratuitous evils of the PLO. Yasir Arafat, whose poor media image is probably beyond repair, is the ranking figure in this cluster of motifs whose basic message is that, if they exist at all, the Palestinians are both marginal and entirely to blame for their misfortunes.

Making his accusation excruciatingly specific, he rattles off a long list of mainstream and in some cases even center-left media sources (CBS, NBC, ABC, PBS, *The New York Times*, *The Washington Post*, *The New Yorker*, *The New York Review of Books*, *The New Republic*, *Commentary*, *Foreign Affairs*, *The American Scholar*, *Partisan Review*, *Policy Review*, *The Atlantic Monthly*, *Dissent*, the *New Criterion*, *Midstream*, *Tikkun*, *Moment*, and *The American Spectator*) and claims that no "sustained, meaningful, and undeterred" exceptions to what he's describing can be found at *any* of them. Nor is this a matter of the media *ignoring* the scholars. He rattles off an extensive list of Middle East "experts" who regularly appear in mainstream media sources to bolster the dominant narrative—one of whom, of course, is Bernard Lewis. He uses Lewis (along with the philosopher Ernest Gellner) in a passage vividly illustrating what Said means by Orientalism:

I could supply you with a list of people who either could do a better or more informed job, or whose efforts to do the job have been systematically rebuffed. The US media is, I would say, much more predisposed to hearing Bernard Lewis explain the TWA hijacking by a long, abstract, general account of Shia history until the Middle Ages, than in hearing about the widespread, ongoing debate between nationalists and supporters of Islamic tendencies, or between various factions within the Islamic tendency itself. The media is prone to welcome, I would say it is primed for, Gellner's theses that Muslims are a nuisance and viscerally anti-Semitic, that their culture and politics can be discussed in thousands of words without a single reference to people, periods, or events. The media is far less interested in discovering whether there is a significant correlation between assertions about Islam based exclusively on classical texts on the one hand, and on the other what Muslims in various countries, belonging to various classes, different genders, in differing social systems, actually do.

Lewis's debate partner, Leon Wieseltier, is next. He acknowledges that Western journalists, like all journalists, are often shallow and ignorant in their discussion of distant places and the people who live there. This is true when Western journalists discuss Arabs and Muslims, but it's no less true when they talk about Indians or Africans, and anyway Arab and Muslim journalists are just as shallow and ignorant when they talk about Westerners.

Sometimes people in different cultures are prejudiced against each other, of course, but often they just don't know very much about one another. Still, he says, there are honorable exceptions like—and yes, Wieseltier really says this—Thomas Friedman. I've read academic philosophy papers that will say that some logical derivation can be left "as an exercise to the reader." In the same spirit, I'll recommend that any reader who's curious about what the exact phenomenon that Edward Said is describing looks like when it's spread over several hundred pages should track down a copy of Friedman's 1989 doorstopper *From Beirut to Jerusalem*. Enjoy.

Anyway, Wieseltier says, the media also has biases against Israel. Israel's war in Lebanon was pretty bad but it was portrayed in the media as being a more terrible thing than it was. And what about the "common prejudice of the American media that Israel should vacate all or most of the West Bank as soon as it can"? Of course, he too thinks Israel should get out of the West Bank, but that's not the point. The point is that it's a prejudice, and one that's against Israel. (Update: In the thirty-five years that have passed since the shootout at the

MESA Corral, Israel has continued to rule over the West Bank, incorporating it into its own territory in every way except for giving the Palestinians who live there Israeli citizenship, and the vast majority of mainstream media coverage in the United States is still quite friendly to Israel. I suppose most journalists do, though, harbor some vague "prejudice" that Israel really should sooner or later get around to ending this egregious violation of both international law and the elementary norms of human decency.)

The final speaker, on Team Said, is a self-described "transplanted English radical" named Christopher Hitchens. Sadly, the original film was damaged at just the point where Hitch starts to speak, although it comes back before he's done. The YouTube version I watched solves this problem by splicing in an actor reading from the transcript of the missing part of Hitchens's remarks. (The transcript of the entire debate was published in *The Journal of Palestine Studies* in 1987.) This may have been the best solution available, but it makes for a jarring and disappointing experience. Hitchens's voice and delivery were important parts of what made him so effective as the rhetorical equivalent of an MMA fighter. I've suggested elsewhere that during the final years of his life when his arguments (at least on some subjects) were weakest, his voice and delivery created a "Christopher Hitchens Effect" that covered over the defects. Whether or not you think this was a fair accusation, there's no denying that his voice and delivery were a large part of what made him such a pleasure to watch in debates.

Even the transcript, though, shows Hitch building his case with his usual flair. He talks about Joan Peters' book *From Time Immorial*, a historically illiterate screed in which Peters tried to show that there was no such thing as a Palestinian people with a real claim on even the West Bank. The reception of this book in the United States "ranged from the respectful to the moist and the adoring." Only after extensive takedowns had been published elsewhere (including in the Israeli press) did some half-hearted reconsiderations start to appear in the American media. He contrasts this with a book called *The Fateful Triangle* written by one of 1980s Hitchens's heroes, "Professor Noam Chomsky." *The Fateful Triangle* was an "unrivaled" treatment of Israel's war in Lebanon—long, "densely footnoted," and not incidentally written by an American Jew with an "international scholarly reputation." Not only did it not get any "moist and adoring" reviews, it wasn't reviewed at all in the *New York Times*, or in Wieseltier's magazine *The New Republic*, in Hitchens's own magazine, *The Nation*, or in any of the other magazines "on the list that even Edward, with his speed and dash of delivery, didn't have time to complete reading."

Oh, and speaking of *The New Republic*:

> Where did the following appear? The description of a play at the American Repertory Theater in this town: "The universalist prejudice of our culture prepared us for this play's Arab, a crazed Arab to be sure, but crazed in the distinctive ways of his culture. He is intoxicated by language, cannot discern between fantasy and reality, abhors compromise, always blames others for his predicament and, in the end, lances the painful boil of his frustrations in a pointless, though momentarily gratifying, act of bloodlust." That is a signed comment by the owner and editor of *The New Republic*. I disagree with you, Leon; I'm sorry, I don't believe that could appear about an Indian or an African in any other magazine in this country.

In the closing statements, Wieseltier huffs and puffs about Hitchens's "dishonesty" and Lewis does him one better by claiming that Said is somehow attacking "truth and objectivity" even as regulative ideals, but neither is able to mount much of a defense on the extremely specific points made by the team of Said and Hitchens. It should be obvious to any fair-minded viewer that Wieseltier and Lewis are just wrong to deny, and Hitchens and Said are right to assert, that Western media coverage, abetted by the services of an array of Islamophobic academic experts, traffics in crudely essentialist ideas about Muslims, Arabs, and in particular Palestinians. To the extent that this is what was at issue, it's an open and shut case. But to the extent that the underlying issue ("The *Scholars*, the Media, and the Middle East") was about Said's academic views, it's worth noting that a far better critique than anything Lewis or Wieseltier had to offer in 1986 existed then and has been further developed since. Moreover, it's a critique that Hitchens himself *should have agreed with*, given his stated lifelong allegiance to the materialist theory of history.

Building on the earlier work of Marxist scholars like Sadiq Jalal Al-Azm and Aijaz Ahmad, Vivek Chibber lays out this critique in an essay called "Orientalism and its Afterlives" in the socialist theoretical journal *Catalyst*. Chibber doesn't accuse Said of hating truth and objectivity or wanting everyone to eat raw dough and crab apples. He opens by talking about the very real virtues of Said and his most famous book:

Few works have had a greater influence on the current Left than Edward Said's *Orientalism*. In the first instance, it has become the lodestone for critical scholarship around the colonial experience and imperialism. But, more expansively, in its status as a founding text of post-colonial studies, its imprint can be discerned across the moral sciences—in race studies, history, cultural theory, and even political economy. Indeed, it is hard to think of many books that have had a greater influence on critical scholarship over the past half century. There are some respects in which Said's placement of colonialism at the center of the modern era has had a salutary effect, not just on scholarship, but also on politics.

Even as the Left went into retreat in the neoliberal era, even as working-class parties either shrank in influence or were absorbed into the mainstream, the centrality of anti-imperialism surprisingly remained close to the center of Left discourse—an achievement in no small part attributable to Said's great book.

Precisely because it's been so important, Chibber insists, the contemporary Left should take it seriously enough to take a hard look at Said's arguments. One half of Said's analysis (roughly, the half in dispute between Said and the Lewis-Wieseltier team) is suggested in a passage Chibber quotes from *Orientalism* describing the claims made by defenders of Western colonialism:

> Orientals have never understood the meaning of self-government the way "we" do. When some Orientals oppose racial discrimination while others practice it, you say "they're all Orientals at bottom" and class interest, political circumstances, economic factors are totally irrelevant... History, politics, and economics do not matter. Islam is Islam, the Orient is the Orient, and please take all your ideas about a left and a right wing, revolutions, and change back to Disneyland.

Said's point here is that essentializing "Eastern" cultures as a kind of Oriental Hive Mind served to justify colonialism—which was itself, of course, undertaken for straightforwardly economic reasons. (To shamelessly recycle a line from my last book, the British Empire didn't conquer India for the purpose of "culturally appropriating" its curry.) The "scientific" work produced by Western scholars in the colonial period played a significant role in propping up this kind of nonsense, just as in more recent times the Bernard Lewises of the world have lent their scholarly credentials to the mainstream media for the sake of reinforcing crude essentialism about the "ancient" roots of terrorism for the purposes of rationalizing American foreign policy.

This part of Said's analysis isn't particularly original—it's a pretty standard left analysis of colonialism—but Chibber grants that the "erudition and literary quality" Said brought to the task of laying it all out was unique. However many other scholars had made the same points, "no one had made them with the same panache and, hence, to the same effect."

Chibber's objection is to the part of Said's argument that was far more original, and that unfortunately has influenced the direction of much of subsequent "post-colonial studies." This part of the argument reversed the order of explanation, tracing the roots of modern Orientalist discourse to exoticizing portrayals of Eastern cultures found as far back as ancient Greek writings and portraying Orientalism as a *cause* of colonialism as much as a consequence of it.

Chibber objects to this aspect of Said's work, which posits a "continuity in Western discourse from Homer to Richard Nixon," and to Said's claim that the Western impulse to dominate the East arose at least in large part *out of* that discourse, for several reasons. First, if this discourse is as pervasive across as many different societies over the course of as many centuries as all that, it sounds more than a little like Said is postulating an Occidental Hive Mind that's *essentially* Orientalist. Second, if ancient Greek or even medieval Christian sources *hadn't* portrayed distant cultures in crude and inaccurate ways, that would have been remarkable. Arab, Persian, and Indian texts from the same time periods "are no less parochial in their descriptions of Europe and its people, and no less prone to generalize across time and space." If, as Said himself sometimes acknowledges, this urge to generalize in absurd ways about other cultures is hardly unique to the West, it's unclear how the earlier attitudes Said refers to as "latent" Orientalism are supposed to even partially explain the rise of colonialism in a few *particular* modern nations. Finally, the political implications are disturbing.

Conventional accounts of colonial expansion had typically adverted to the role of interest groups, classes, and state managers as its animating force. For Marxists, it had been capitalists; for nationalists, it had been "British interests"; for liberals, it was overly ambitious political leaders. What all these explanations had in common was the central role that they accorded to material interests as the motivating factor in colonial rule. But if, in fact, Orientalism as a body of thought propels its believers toward the accumulation of territories, then it is not interests that drive the project, but a deeply rooted cultural disposition—a discourse, to put it in contemporary jargon.

If the Marxists are correct, not just about classical colonialism but about contemporary neo-colonialism, the solution is relatively clear. Empire-building serves the interests of a wealthy minority, not the working-class majority, and this simple insight points to the possibility of that majority being mobilized for an anti-imperial political project. This might be extremely difficult in practice, but it's not inconceivable. If, on the other hand, the culprit is some deep feature of Western culture, the solution is... what? Perhaps getting some Middle East Studies equivalent of popular "anti-racism trainer" Robin DiAngelo to conduct Anti-Orientalism Trainings? Failing this, it's easy to see how those on the Left most influenced by the dubious half of Said's analysis often end up as apologists for any unsavory force anywhere in the world that acts as any kind of local counterweight to the power of the American Empire. If there's no hope for an anti-imperialist agenda triumphing *within* America or other Western power, then there's nothing left for Western anti-imperialists to do but carry water for any tinpot dictator, sketchy "liberation army" or even rival global power that can at least check the reach of American power.

Of course, it would be a little much to expect Christopher Hitchens to have critiqued Said on Chibber-ish grounds in 1986. The earliest version of this critique I know of came from Sadiq Jalal Al-Azm, who published an article called "Orientalism and orientalism in reverse" in 1980. I have no idea if Hitchens had ever heard of Al-Azm. If he had, he might recognize a kindred spirit. Al-Azm had been imprisoned in Lebanon ten years before writing his critique of *Orientalism* for writing a materialist tract called *Naqd al-Fikr al-Dini (Critique of Religious Thought)*. But even if he had been aware of Al-Azm's writing, Hitchens might not have been receptive to the point.

For one thing, Said was being attacked in 1986 not by Marxist scholars upset that Said's critique of Orientalism was insufficiently materialist but by reactionary buffoons like Bernard Lewis and Leon Wieseltier who were upset about everything that Said got *right*. Hitch might well have calculated that esoteric intra-left disputes were beside the point in that context.

Beyond this, Hitchens attacking Edward Said in 1986 would have been an unthinkable display of personal disloyalty. Said and Hitchens were then and would remain both literary and political allies and warm personal friends—until they were finally driven apart in the aftermath of September 11.

II.    Hitchens and John Judis vs. Harry Biswanger and John Ridpath: "Capitalism vs. Socialism" (1986)

Eleven days before he and Said debated Wieseltier and Lewis, Hitchens was on another debate stage, laying out five propositions that he saw as "necessary but not sufficient" prerequisites for any kind of socialist political project.

It is necessary to hold, firstly, that all divisions of class, nation, race, and sex are in the last resort man-made and can be man-unmade, are in no sense part of a divine or natural ordinance, and that we are members, like it or no, of one race, the human race.

That civilization is in fact, second, a cooperative enterprise, whether the cooperation was coerced, as it was in most of recorded history, or voluntary, as has occasionally been found and can still be found in our century—but that it is a cooperative enterprise cannot be denied. There is no other means, that's to say, of civilization.

Third, that the limits of creative endeavor are set by the limits of nature, and very few human actions can therefore in the last instance be said to be entirely private. The Earth is in point of fact our common treasury, as the English Levelers used to say in the Puritan Revolution, hoping that it was so. It is in fact the case, and again whether we like it or not, and whether we care to treat it as such or not.

Fourth, that there is no God and no supernatural, that this recognition obliges us morally to maximize the felicity of the one life that we are permitted.

And fifth that the principle of from each according to his ability or her ability, to each according to his or her need is an easily realizable one, prefigured already in human society by the working principles of the bourgeois family. That unique engine of thrift, enterprise, [and] the transmission of morality operates precisely on the principle of from each according to his or her ability and to each according to his or her need. There is in fact no other way that a family could decently or possibly be run.

Hitchens goes on to talk about various empirical claims that he thinks are enough, when combined with the five opening propositions, to get all the way to socialist political conclusions.

These are standard claims about history and class struggle that should be familiar to anyone who's read a little Marx.

At one point Hitchens uses the example of donating blood to show what a socialist ethos looks like. The donor isn't really engaged in an act of self-sacrifice, but simply acting out the natural human impulse toward cooperation and mutual aid. One of his opponents on the pro-capitalist side, Harry Biswanger, responds that he doesn't have a problem with *voluntarily* donating blood, but he would be against the state taking people's blood by force even to save the lives of dying people in hospitals who desperately need transfusions.

Hitchens's next turn to speak doesn't come for a while, and this thread of discussion will be long since lost by then, but a good reply would have been to borrow George Kateb's response to the libertarian philosopher Robert Nozick and insist that the external economic resources that might be owned by some capitalist are importantly different from the blood in the capitalist's body, and that they just don't have as strong a claim to the former as they do to the latter. "I find it impossible," Kateb said, "to conceive of us as having nerve endings in every dollar of our estates."

Hitchens's partner on the pro-socialist side is *New Republic* contributor John Judis. While both Judis and Hitchens make a few comments over the course of the debate suggesting that the most promising path *to* socialism is an evolutionary one starting with social democratic reforms within capitalism, Hitchens's understanding of what the fully socialist end point of that process would look like does seem to be much more boldly utopian. Judis has a grounded vision of feasible socialism in which some market mechanisms would still exist side-by-side with democratic control of the means of production. Hitchens's point about "from each, to each" suggests that the entire economy can be reorganized on the model of a kind of giant family.

To see how much more radical the implications of *that* are, think about an actual family sitting down to dinner together. Whether this is a traditional patriarchal family where mom does all the cooking or a modern egalitarian family where such domestic duties are shared, *whoever* spent the last hour stirring pasta isn't going to demand payment from everyone else at the table. The very suggestion that market mechanisms be introduced in this context would be regarded as at least eccentric (and probably disturbing) by everyone concerned.

On the pro-capitalist side, Biswanger and his debate partner Johns Ridpath are both devotees of the "objectivist" philosophy of the novelist Ayn Rand. This means that, however much they might have disagreed with him about socialism, Biswanger and Ridpath were definitely on board with Hitchens's third proposition.

In fact, Randians typically argue that *because* there is no God and you have only one life to live, the only goal you have any reason to care about is living up to your individual potential. Rand was careful to explain that this doesn't mean that you should act like a barbarian, killing and raping and robbing according to your passing whims. Instead, she thought that a man's true interests lie in flowering as a rational and creative being by developing his talents and abilities and living the best life that he can. (She always said "man" and "he," and I'll follow her convention in explaining her ideas.) She thought that the interests of rational beings, understood this way, always coincide, since everyone has an interest in peaceful ground rules for free competition among individuals.

Crucially, though, Rand's vision of morality didn't have any room for the idea that anyone has a moral reason to put aside their individual interests *to any degree whatsoever* out of consideration for the interests of others. If taxing some small part of the fortunes of the wealthiest people would pay for universal tuition-free higher education, for example—thus giving people who otherwise couldn't afford college a better shot at living up to *their* individual potentials—this would be an unacceptable imposition on the liberty of wealthy taxpayers.

This is the aspect of her views that's the hardest for nearly everyone else to swallow. Rand called her philosophy "objectivism" because she thought everyone else was denying objective reality—roughly, the reality summed up in Hitchens's third proposition—but if the relevant set of objective facts includes the fact that everyone else in the world besides me *also* has only one life to live, shouldn't this give me at least some reason to take *their* interests into account, either in my individual behavior or when I think about what kind of society is worth fighting for? If most people don't have a voice or a vote in deciding what happens during the eight hours a day they're at work—and remember it's only *eight* because of state intervention brought about by past workers' struggles—and indeed if many people stay in jobs or even marriages they hate because they don't want to lose their or their spouse's employer health insurance, this means they're less capable of pursuing their own individual dreams than they would be in a society that took care of everyone's basic needs and extended democracy to the workplace. Given the underlying normative premise that the attempts of individuals to attain whatever kind of excellence they might be capable of attaining are made more urgent by the fact that this life is all there is—no do-overs and no heavenly rewards for noble suffering—shouldn't we try to achieve a society where everyone can flourish to a reasonable extent, even if achieving that goal means curbing some of the property rights of the wealthy and powerful? If Jeff Bezos, for example, could no longer afford to own his own spaceship, he would still be capable of a great deal of individual flourishing.

The reason the Biswangers and Ridpaths of the world don't see things this way is that they don't think that *everyone* has a reason to care about *everyone*'s flourishing but just that *you* have a reason to care about *your* flourishing. In other words, despite Rand's caveat about the difference between a rational man who properly understands what pursuing individual excellence means and a barbarian who loots and pillages as the fancy takes him, there's a sense in which, on the intellectual ground floor, "objectivists" like Rand and Ridpath and Biswanger really do think like Douglas Wilson's imaginary atheist who sees no reason to regret his crimes because he got away with them. This hypothetical villain and the all-too-real Ayn Rand both think that no one has any reason to advance anyone else's interests if that isn't in their interest.

Randians have two strategies for making all this seem less monstrous than it is. The first is to accuse their opponents of being "collectivists" not just in the sense of advocating collective ownership of the means of production but in the sense of thinking that morality is about the abstract good of "collectives" rather than the real lives of individual human beings. The "collectivists" described by Rand and her followers allegedly want to ruthlessly sacrifice individuals for the "greater good" of collective entities. Whether the collective entity in question is "the white race" or "the international working class," Randians allege, the underlying moral error is the same.

The other strategy is to characterize all moral theories other than Rand's own as variations of "altruism," which objectivists don't define the way that everybody else does, as acting unselfishly on behalf of others, but as the view that people should *only* act in this way and that *ever* acting for your own sake to pursue your own projects and live up to your own potential is morally wrong. Rhetorically, it's a good strategy— her version of rational egoism starts to sound a lot better if the only options are that or a life of monkish self-abnegation.

The problem in both cases is that these are wildly inaccurate summaries of the history of philosophy. There might be some truth to the charge of "collectivism" when it comes to some *particular* moral theories but "altruism" in Rand's sense is almost entirely a straw man.

Classical utilitarians think that morality is all about maximizing happiness and minimizing suffering, and that it doesn't matter how that happiness or suffering is distributed between individual human (or indeed non-human) brains. Avoiding a given quantity of suffering has the same moral significance whether it's localized in one mind or each of a hundred people is experiencing one percent of that much suffering. This could be seen as a real example of moral (as opposed to economic) "collectivism"—treating questions of happiness or suffering as if it was all being experienced by one giant entity. And perhaps some of the most fanatical versions of religious morality might shade into what Randians (and only Randians) call "altruism"—although even there, religious believers often say that individual talents are gifts from God that shouldn't be squandered.

At any rate, when it comes to *secular* moral philosophy, we have one theory (utilitarianism) that is collectivist but not altruist, none that are altruist but not collectivist, and none that are both. When we turn to utilitarianism's most important competitor, we find that Kant's most memorable formulation of his Categorical Imperative commands that no one treat "humanity, *whether in the person or yourself or another*," as "merely a means to an end" rather than "an end in itself." Sacrificing an individual for the greater good—by, for example, pushing her onto a trolley track—would violate this principle if anything would.

A striking way to see the gap between real Kantianism and Rand's caricature of that and other moral philosophies being "altruistic" in her sense is to look at the four examples Kant gives in his *Groundwork of the Metaphysics of Morals* of actions that violate the Categorical Imperative. Two of them have to do with Categorical Imperative-derived duties to other people, but the other two are examples of people violating CI-derived duties to themselves—a man who violates the duty to preserve his life by committing suicide, and another who fails to develop his talents.

In the twentieth century, John Rawls formulated a theory of political justice loosely inspired by some of Kant's insights. Rawls thought that the way to tell whether any person is being treated unjustly by social institutions is to consider whether they would have signed off on those institutions from the "original position." Imagine that you knew everything there was to know about every empirical issue that would be relevant to deciding on a set of political and economic arrangements. You knew, for example, whether enacting "hate speech" laws would lead a society down a slippery slope to other kinds of speech restrictions. You'd know whether it would be possible to have a fully planned economy without leading to empty shelves at the grocery store *a la* the USSR. Everyone in the Original Position would also know that you'd have to live in the society you were designing. Crucially, though, you wouldn't know what your position would be in that society—whether you would be poor or rich, black or white, male or female, and so on.

Rawls's theory of justice is neither "collectivist" nor "altruist" in Rand's sense of those terms. Imagine, for example, that there was some very efficient way to engineer a slave system such that only one percent of the population had to be enslaved to serve the needs of the other ninety-nine percent. Rawls has an easy time explaining why this would be horrifically unjust. No one designing a society from behind his "veil of ignorance" would risk being born into this tiny slave caste. The unit of moral evaluation here is the individual, and Rawls places a great deal of emphasis on everyone's right to pursue their own particular "life plan."

Many of the consequences of Rawls's view are straightforward enough—no one who didn't know whether they would be born black or white would endorse the racial laws of Apartheid South Africa, for example—but in his original book on the subject, *A Theory of Justice*, Rawls leaves open the question of whether people in the original position would choose capitalism (with suitable welfare-state modifications to alleviate the conditions of the worst off) or some sort of collective ownership of the means of production. He sees this as an empirical question and holds open the possibility that people in the original position might select capitalism if it turned out that the worst-off people in a capitalist society plagued by economic inequality would be better off than the citizens of a far more egalitarian but economically dysfunctional socialist alternative.

By the time he wrote his end-of-career book *Justice as Fairness: A Restatement*, though, Rawls had decided that no version of capitalism, no matter how robust a social safety net it was combined with, could satisfy the requirements of his theory of justice. Being a Swedish worker is better than being an American worker, but even Swedish workplaces operate far too much like petty dictatorships on a day-to-day basis. Even in Sweden, it takes the average CEO less than a week to earn the average annual salary of a Swedish worker. Whether society-designers in the Original Position would choose a fully planned economy or some form of market socialism might be an open empirical question, but it's just not plausible that they would choose capitalism.

The reason I bring all this up isn't that I think Rawls's theory is the last philosophical word on economic justice. The great twentieth century Marxist analytic philosopher G.A. Cohen, for example, had some insightful criticisms of the limits of Rawls's approach. The point is just this: At least in the Anglo-American tradition, Rawls is universally regarded as the most important political philosopher of the twentieth century...and even this very short tour of Rawls's theory should be more than enough to show that objectivists are spouting nonsense when they claim that the only options are to fanatically defend capitalist property rights or be guilty of moral "collectivism" and (what they call) "altruism." Everyone on the bottom end of capitalist economic hierarchies is individually experiencing an injustice. Being a victim of that injustice gives you one reason (and your moral concern for everyone else in the same circumstance gives you another) to remedy this situation through working-class solidarity and *collective* action.

As Hitchens forcefully shows during his rebuttal to the objectivists in the second round of the debate, Biswanger and Ridpath are also being deeply sloppy when they accuse him and Judis of wanting to sacrifice individual freedom for the sake of the collective by wanting to bring the means of production into social ownership. Biswanger and Ridpath's claims that socialism=coercion and capitalism=property rights=freedom are wrong on both normative and empirical levels. As Marx and Engels recognized in *The Communist Manifesto*, "the free development of each" requires "the free development of all." In other words—although neither Hitch nor of course Marx puts it this way—the liberation of the working class from capitalist domination is a necessary condition for as many people as possible being freed to the greatest possible extent to pursue their own individual life plans. Hitchens also points out that Biswanger and Ridpath's generalizations about capitalism and socialism are historically illiterate.

The history of capitalism and even more so, it should be said, the history of capitalism in its imperialist phase, is the history of expropriation—is the history of the robbery of private property from millions and millions of people. Marx, observing this process in *The Communist Manifesto*, remarks on the tremendous advances in productivity and technique and innovation that were thereby enabled, but he does point to the fact that many, many people who hitherto had owned land, property, and so on, were expropriated, collectivized, and made into the modern proletariat. He thought the price was worth paying. He thought capitalism *was* an advance over what had gone before...but let no one tell you that capitalism cannot co-exist with the expropriation of private property.

As he goes on to say, even the process by which peasants in the imperial heartland were dispossessed of their land at the dawn of capitalism was a pleasant stroll through the park compared to, for example, the way the British Empire plundered places like India for raw materials for British factories. Turning to the twentieth century, he starts talking about fascism. Objectivists in the audience boo him as he patiently explains that, no, he isn't saying that capitalism is always and everywhere fascist— but fascism damn well *is* a form that capitalism can take and has in certain circumstances taken, and we can say more generally that "there is no limit" to the violence that will be perpetrated by capitalists who see their profits threatened.

The obvious late twentieth century example of what Hitchens is talking about here would be Chile, where the democratic socialist government of Salvador Allende was deposed in a US-backed coup. The American Secretary of State at the time, one Henry Kissinger, remarked that he didn't see why Chile should be allowed to "go communist" simply because the voters of that country were "irresponsible."

In the subsequent discussion, Biswanger and Ridpath distance themselves from the record of what could be called Actually Existing Capitalism (AEC). As debaters with positions like theirs so often do, they awkwardly navigate between claiming that only a hypothetical libertarian utopia would count as real capitalism and trying to take credit for the many achievements of the "approximation" of capitalism that came into existence in the modern world. The unsavory stuff, of course, can be blamed on the "statist" elements of AEC—much the way that devout Christians who think the good parts of the world testify to the glory of the Creator blame the bad parts on original sin.

To be fair, Hitchens and Judis are no more interested in defending Actually Existing Socialism as it then existed— assuming that Tony Cliff's "state capitalism" analysis is wrong— in the USSR. Judis talks about Hegel's concept of the "cunning of history," which he says means that historical outcomes aren't simply the sum of the intentions of individual people, and uses this to explain that the mere fact of some regime latching onto a label that was historically popular among working-class people doesn't tell you much about its true nature. In the same spirit (but with more eloquence) Hitchens says that "no one bothers to counterfeit a bad currency," and "the claim of so many people who don't deserve it to the socialist title gives one hope for a more enlightened application of the idea in the non-capitalist future."

This version of Hitchens sounds in almost every way like a very orthodox Marxist. He sounds that way when he talks about history and he sounds that way when he talks about contemporary politics and he certainly sounds that way when he talks about religion. At one point in the Q&A someone asks if Jesus was a socialist. Judis hedges a bit, saying that he's personally on the "Judeo-" side of the "Judeo-Christian" tradition but that he thinks some versions of Christianity are compatible with socialism. The objectivists say that Jesus probably *was* a socialist and that they find Christianity and socialism to be equally rooted in a life-denying ethos of self-sacrifice and thus equally abhorrent. Hitchens's response to *that* is exactly what you would expect it to be.

III.   Hitchens and Jesse Jackson vs. Hadley Arkes and Stephen Markman: "The death penalty should be abolished" (1997)

Eleven years later, Hitchens is at a debate on the death penalty co-sponsored by *The Nation*. Despite their metaphysical disagreements, his debate partner is the Reverend Jesse Jackson—whose presidential campaign Hitch supported in 1988. Hitchens and Jackson are facing off against a pair of ghouls from *The National Review*.

The debate is moderated by former New York City Mayor Ed Koch, but parts of Hitch's opening salvo sound like an educational presentation he might have given to an Oxford branch meeting of the International Socialists in 1970. He starts by saying that he's going to explain why death penalty abolition is important to "those of us on this side of the house" whose politics are ultimately directed at the creation of a "classless society." Not only are he and Jackson opposed to human sacrifice, Hitch says, they object to "a system that requires it."

Discussing a recent execution in Florida when the electric chair malfunctioned and the victim was immolated in a particularly grotesque way, he notes that this is not a new problem. Prison officials there call the chair "Old Sparky." He quotes a prosecutor who publicly said that the fact that the execution equipment in Florida didn't seem to be working properly gave criminals an extra reason not to murder anyone in the state. Is the picture starting to become clear? These displays of public cruelty are ultimately all about reinforcing hierarchy by displaying raw state power.

All the statistical evidence shows that the death penalty is a racist institution. Hitchens calls it a "legacy of the time when sharp reminders were needed of who was running the show." He warns, though, that opponents of capital punishment shouldn't place too much emphasis on this point. It could be argued that the racial disparities in execution statistics could only show "a problem with racism," not a problem with judicially killing people *per se*. Other penalties are applied in racist ways too. "'Very well,' it could be said, 'let us have a non-racist application of the human sacrifice principle.'"

He goes on to disown another argument typically made by his side—one, he says, that seems to impress so many liberals that if you make it, you will "infallibly" have your letter to the editor printed by *The New York Times*. "If we kill killers," the letter-writers always fret, "that makes the state like them." Hitchens ridicules the concern that the American state is noble enough to start with that, if not for the death penalty, there *would* be a moral difference between "our government" and a gang of murderers. "Well, excuse me," he says, this is a state that has been training "murderers, torturers and death squad convenors all across Central America" for decades. It's a state that has a vast stockpile of thermonuclear weaponry with which it reserves the option of wiping out human civilization if diplomatic negotiations get really tense. It's the largest exporter of conventional weapons in the history of the world.

Killing prisoners is objectionable, but not because the American imperial state wouldn't be plenty murderous without capital punishment on the home front. It's objectionable because it's not reversible, which other penalties are, "even if they've been applied by a racist system that never punishes the rich." And it's objectionable as a matter of principle, because no state should have "the power of life and death over its citizens."

The ultimate goal, he says, is a system in which the rule of some men over other men has been replaced by what Marx called "the administration of things." This is the idea that in a sufficiently advanced society where people no longer had clashing economic interests, any remaining entity bearing even a family resemblance to governments as we currently know them would exist not to enforce relations of power but simply to make sure the machinery of social coordination kept running smoothly. Presumably, even if capitalism is abolished tomorrow, it's going to take a long, long time to get *there*. In the meantime, though, he doesn't think any government should be trusted with the despotic power to "order you to die."

IV. Hitchens vs. Hitchens at Conway Hall: "The abolition of Britain" (1999)

The initial joke about "comrades" is made by *Peter* Hitchens. Martin Amis will get that detail wrong, and Christopher won't correct him.

It's an easy mistake to make. Christopher really does have a jovial habit of addressing every audience in every hall with the salutation "comrades," regardless of their political makeup. This will remain a staple of his crowd work for the rest of his life, even when he's debating the existence of God in front of audiences full of Southern evangelicals. He probably even uses the word half a dozen times over the course of *this* debate. But the initial riff on how Conway Hall events used to be full of "comrades" comes from Peter, and he's using it to build to a very un-Christopher-ish conclusion.

Both brothers were members of the International Socialists in the era of mass street protests against the Vietnam War. These days they have entirely different attitudes toward their political pasts. Peter seems to have forgotten the difference between Trotskyism and Stalinism. He also doesn't appear to see much distinction between Marxism and Blairism.

Peter's view is that "the Left" has always hated Britain and Britishness. The only reason they supported the war against Hitler is that the Wehrmacht invaded the Soviet Union. And, he says, the "old comrades" who used to fill this hall have never really gone away. Ex-radicals are running the Labour government currently in power, and they never really gave up their desire to "abolish Britain." Now that Britain's in an increasingly centralized European Union, they finally have their chance. They can carry out the unchanging imperatives of cosmopolitan internationalism by transferring British sovereignty to bureaucrats in Brussels.

At least, Peter says, Christopher is *honest* about his desire to abolish the monarchy and surrender "the Irish part of the country" to the IRA. It's clear to Peter that the Blairites and their friends in the EU are working toward the same goals but without the courage to openly proclaim it.

Christopher's affection for his brother is obvious. As he starts his response, he seems to want to find things to praise about this stridently reactionary presentation. He definitely pulls a few punches. Peter leaned heavily on George Orwell's sometimes colorful expressions of frustration with the eccentricities of his fellow leftists for evidence that the Left has always hated all things British. Christopher, who revered Orwell, doesn't take his opportunity point that (a) Orwell was a lifelong socialist, who (b) couldn't be accused of only supporting the war out of solidarity with Stalin's Russia. Oh, and (c) Orwell wrote in 1947 "a socialist United States of Europe seems to me the only worthwhile political objective today." Christopher will quote that line in a couple of years in *Why Orwell Matters*.

As the reply goes on, his fraternal tenderness slips. Christopher starts having some fun at his brother's expense. At the Oxford Union, he says, they were told that it was important that you be able to summarize your opponent's argument as if it were your own. In this case, though, there are a few things he doesn't get. He doesn't worry, as his brother seems to, that the Tory Party isn't conservative enough, that the Labour Party isn't radical enough, or that venerable British institutions like the monarchy and the Church of England "aren't absurd enough."

Christopher praises the EU on several grounds. It's provided a framework of international cooperation that helped resolve the conflict in Northern Ireland and stopped "the Basque question" in Spain from spilling over into a similar level of violence. It's provided multiple countries on the European continent with an incentive to enact democratic reforms. (The

EU refuses to take dictatorships as new members.) It's very good, he thinks, that people denied justice in British courts can appeal to European courts. Its very existence as a modest counterweight to the American colossus undermines the so-called "special relationship" between the UK and the US that led to such horrors as Margaret Thatcher's chumminess with the murderous Chilean dictator Augusto Pinochet. Christopher even suggests that so-called "Euroskeptics" like Peter want to turn the UK into something like an "offshore Serbia"—a country "resentful" when others "interfere in its affairs" to try to enforce standards of human rights.

In the subsequent exchange, Peter (and then multiple members of the audience) press Christopher on the weakest part of his defense of the EU. What about the "democratic deficit"—all the decisions made not by the elected European Parliament but by appointed commissioners? Christopher's response is that the European Commission is hardly the only powerful institution whose ruling officials aren't up for popular election. The same is true of the Bank of England, the monarchy, and "the boards of multinational corporations." Some on the Left, he says, are Euroskeptical in their own way because they say the EU is a club for wealthy capitalists. Well, he says, *it is*, but that's a non sequitur in this context because so is the UK. The "struggle for democracy" will have to be waged one way or the other, but it's better for it to be waged on a Europe-wide terrain than a parochial British one.

Parts of his argument sound like something the 1986 version of Hitchens might have said. But it's telling that, while he makes a few hand-wavey references to struggles to expand democracy waged by someone-or-other, he says almost nothing about the organized working class. The only explicit reference to that social force comes in an aside about how Peter is more honest than most Euroskeptical Tories in his willingness to admit that Thatcher was the one who really destroyed the Britain of their youth by taking on a variety of powerful institutions, including the trade unions.

V.   Hitchens, Alexander Pires, and Matt Brown vs. Glen Loury, Deroy Murdock, and Amy Margolius: "Should reparations be paid to the descendants of slaves?" (2001)

Three months after 9/11, Christopher Hitchens is in Boston, arguing that black Americans should be paid reparations. So many people are speaking that the event sometimes feels more like an anthology of speeches than a debate, but Hitchens's presentation is worth watching on its own as a snapshot of his changing politics.

He pours scorn on the slimy evasions of reactionaries who ask whether black people today aren't actually better off *because* their ancestors were taken from Africa to the United States. Rationalizations this silly, he suggests, are evidence of a guilty conscience.

He reaches back to the controversy about one of his earliest books, on the British Empire's theft of the Elgin Marbles, as an analogy for the "white whine" that greets demands for reparations. He made the case in this book that the marbles be returned to Greece, and many critics responded by asking if he was saying that *every* foreign object in *every* Western museum be returned to its country of origin. Of course, he wasn't saying any such thing. In some countries, local conditions might be such that some artifact is better off in the British Museum. In other cases, the connection between the culture that produced an artifact and the people who now live in the same patch of the world is so tenuous that it's not clear that there's anyone left to reclaim the stolen property. But in this case at least one continuing aspect of the injustice done to the Greeks *can* be rectified. That's what should happen—and the same goes for reparations to the descendants of slaves.

Yes, there are other historical injustices for which no comparable solution is possible. Yes, many of the long-term consequences of slavery, Jim Crow, and the rest can't be erased through reparations alone. But the economic disparities between the descendants of slaves and the descendants of the non-enslaved population *can* be at least partially addressed through reparations. That's what should happen.

He has a strong case against the White Whiners who don't want any sort of redistribution of resources to benefit the descendants of slaves. But it's telling that he isn't moved by the anti-reparations argument that had already been made in print by his friend Adolph Reed.

Hitchens is on the record in multiple places about his admiration for Reed's writing. Reed didn't share Hitchens's post-9/11 politics, but they seem to have remained on good enough terms to have a friendly argument about it all over drinks. Here's Reed in a 2021 article called "The Whole Country is the *Reichstag*":

> Once, in an argument in a Washington, DC bar with Christopher Hitchens during the Afghan War, I asserted that no place in the world had been made better by the presence of the 82nd [Airborne Division], not even Fayetteville, NC, its home base. That stopped Hitchens in his tracks momentarily and prompted a chuckle. Then my son reminded me that the one exception to that dictum had been Oxford, MS in 1962.

Reed's point about reparations is, first, that a focus on racial disparities largely misses the point. America's racial history certainly explains *why* a disproportionate percentage of the black population lives in poverty. Conservatives who deny this and insist that the problem comes from a "culture of dependency" or some such nonsense aren't being serious. America only abolished its system of *de jure* racial apartheid when Reed was a teenager. The question, though, is what would count as justice—demographically appropriate percentages of black and white Americans living in poverty?

Besides, Reed thinks, even if we swallow the dubious assumption that white poverty is justifiable in a way that black poverty isn't, it's hard to see how reparations could happen. Any radical political platform would be extremely difficult to achieve, but if the goal is to redistribute wealth to everyone at the bottom, it's not out of the question that a multiracial working-class movement could one day attract the support of an overall majority of the population. It's much harder to see a scenario where poor and working-class white people would be effectively mobilized to fight for a racially means-tested version of that goal.

Decades later, he reiterates these points in an interview with *Current Affairs* editor Nathan J. Robinson. When Robinson presses him on whether it's ever possible to mobilize people around something that's not in their interest, Reed invokes the classic story "The North Wind and the Sun."

I read Aesop's Fables a lot when I was a kid, and one of my favorite ones was the one about the contest between the wind and the sun, and they were boasting back and forth at each other, and they determined to test their prowess against a wayfarer who was walking along the road, and whichever one could get him to take his coat off would be the more powerful. So the wind blew, and blew, and blew, and no matter how much harder the wind blew, the traveler just kind of pulled his coat more, and more tightly around himself, and when the sun took its turn, and just sort of began to radiate more and more warmth, the traveler eventually took the coat off on his own. My approach to politics, and this goes back to what counts as a movement, and what doesn't, is the project of trying to fasten a broad-based political alliance in which different people and constituencies can not only see a vehicle for pursuing their own interests, but can come to understand that a condition for advancement of their own interests is an equal commitment to advancing their partners' interests. So, from that perspective, I don't understand how we build solidarity by going around the room to stress how profoundly we actually differ from one another.

Reed's critique makes sense if you're thinking strategically about how political change can emerge from the energies of people at the bottom of society. The problem with Hitchens at this point in his career is that he no longer really thinks that way. *The Trial of Henry Kissinger*, for example, was published the same year as the reparations debate. It's a very good book — but the conclusion is all about the legal case for either literally putting Kissinger on trial in the United States or extraditing him to be tried in another country. Disconcertingly, Hitchens writes as if he thinks this might actually happen. Is he that naïve?

It's more that his imagination has narrowed. The American state as a whole can't be put on trial for its crimes, but if he squints in just the right way he can just about see the possibility of that happening to Henry Kissinger — so it's Kissinger as an individual on which he focuses his argument. Similarly, in the debate with his brother, the only hope he really saw for changing the UK for the better was for it to be pulled in better directions by its association with broader European institutions. He's come a long way from the revolutionary excitement of 1971, when he wrote that revolutions involving the "two-thirds of humanity" living in destitution would sweep away both of the world's dominant systems.

VI.  Hitchens and Stephen Fry vs. Ann Widdecombe and Archbishop John Oneiyaken: "The Catholic Church is a force for good in the world" (2009)

In the debate with Peter in 1999, Christopher made a few passing jabs at the Church of England. The second time he debates him, in 2008—we'll go back to that one—a full half of the event is devoted to God and religion. In 2009, Hitchens and Steven Fry are debating a Tory MP (Ann Widdecombe) and a Catholic archbishop (John Oneiyaken) on whether the Catholic Church is "a force for good in the world."

Oneiyaken starts with a bland opening statement enthusing about all the charity work the Church does around the world. Hitchens is the next speaker, and he sounds like a very good prosecutor as he goes through a long list of Catholic atrocities over the centuries, from the massacre of Orthodox Christians in Jerusalem during the Crusades to the condemnation of condom use in Africa during the AIDS crisis. He structures a lot of this by rattling off all the past institutional transgressions of the church that Pope John Paul II had apologized for in (what were then) recent years, and then adds some of his own, like the public burning of Czech religious reformer Jan Hus and the Concordat between the church and Adolph Hitler in the 30s, before getting to the main contemporary item—the pedophilia coverup. "Where," he asks Ann Widdecombe and Archbishop Onaiyekan, "is Cardinal Law?"

For the benefit of anyone too young to catch that reference, I should say that Cardinal Law was the notorious arch-enabler of child-abusing priests in Boston who left the United States in disgrace after the extent of his knowledge of the abuse became public. Two years later, he was appointed by the Pope to a position in the Vatican as Archpriest of the Basilica di Santa Maria Maggiore. He would retire from that job in 2011, but this debate is happening in 2009, and in 2009, "Where is Cardinal

Law?" was a damning question.

Widdecombe goes next, and she points out that laws against pedophilia weren't very harsh until recent decades, and counseling guidelines in secular institutions often relied on unrealistically optimistic assumptions about rehabilitation. When judged by the standards of the *time*, she claims, the Church wasn't unusually bad on this issue. This falls flat when we consider *what specifically* officials like Cardinal Law were up to. Perhaps ignorant ideas about how to handle pedophilia were rampant then. Even so, *covering up instances that had come to light internally*, and continuing to shuffle around abusive priests to new parishes where they would still be in contact with altar boys, was pretty bad even when judged by a generous standard. A chain of secular private schools where high-level administrators were caught doing the equivalent would be in serious trouble.

Widdecombe's strongest point is on the Hitler Question, where she scores some real hits on the historical complexities Hitch left out of his account of the Concordat. Not only did many priests heroically resist, but Pope Pius XII sheltered many Jews at the Vatican. Things are also more complicated than Hitchens portrayed them as being on the Nazi side. Where Hitch pointed out that the regime handed over primary education to the Church as part of a political deal whereby the Catholic political party was dissolved, Widdecombe points out that Catholics had to renounce their ties to the Church to join the SS.

How much of Hitchens's case does any of this really undermine? I'm not sure. It seems like the most historically honest thing to say is that the Nazis and the Church had a messy relationship characterized by a disturbing amount of collaboration on both ends but also by a certain amount of official hostility by the Nazis and a certain amount of resistance by the Church. Real history tends to be more complicated than canned narratives.

Stephen Fry emphasizes the absurdity of the Church's condemnation of his homosexuality. This point ends up being extensively batted back and forth as the debate goes on. Archbishop Onaiyekan does his best to make a "hate the sin, love the sinner" distinction, but this only goes so far in mitigating the obvious cruelty of telling people with "sinful" impulses that they had to be celibate for the rest of their lives. Telling pedophiles, for example, that they can't act on their impulses might be *morally necessary* cruelty—but telling gay people the same thing is just pointlessly cruel.

Returning to a topic Hitchens hit during his opening presentation, Fry says that he's traveled extensively to Uganda for work related to the AIDS crisis. He regards the Church's condemnation of condom use as a moral abomination. Widdecombe responds with a bunch of quotes from non-Catholic experts saying that encouraging condom use wasn't as effective an anti-AIDS strategy as they hoped, but anyone in the audience who's paying close attention to her quotes should be able to tell that the experts' point was that this strategy wasn't *sufficient on its own*, not that condom use didn't considerably diminish the risk of transmitting the virus.

Archbishop Onaiyekan spends most of the debate as the most mild-mannered person on stage, but his back finally seems to be up during his final statement. He emphasizes that Hitchens and Fry's litany of historical horrors doesn't really touch the question of whether the Catholic Church *is* a force for good in the world in the present tense, which is after all what they're supposed to be talking about in this event. Surely all the charity work is the most important way the Church impacts the world *now*.

Narrowing the focus of the debate to the present moment and not defending the first couple of thousand years of the Church's record is an awkward posture for devout Catholics to take. Wasn't this institution supposed to have been guided by the Holy Spirit since its inception? We can also wonder if the archbishop really means to imply that we should do grim Trolley Problem-ish calculations when weighing whether the Church is *presently* more of a force for good or evil overall. On the one hand, pedophilia coverups and dead AIDS victims. On the other hand, billions in charity to feed the global poor.

Even so, Hitchens's response on the question of those billions isn't entirely satisfying. He says the solution to global poverty isn't charity. Fine. But what *is* the solution? "The empowerment of women." The primary things he seems to mean by that phrase are birth control and co-education.

These are both good things, but does Hitchens really believe any amount of either is sufficient to cure structural poverty on a massive scale? Widdecombe rightly pointed out in one of her comments on the condom issue that in traveling to poor countries with high birth rates, women told her again and again that the main reason they had so many children wasn't that the Pope had told them to or that they couldn't find birth control but that *they needed someone to take care of them in their old age.*

Now, Widdecombe doesn't seem to have thought through the implications of this for her own position. If she let herself do *that*, she might come to conclusions incompatible with her continued membership in the Tory Party. But her point is certainly sufficient to show the flaw in Hitch's view. If he'd still been a socialist in 2009, he might have had a better answer.

### VII. Hitchens vs. William Lane Craig: "Does God exist?" (2009)

The Christian analytic philosopher William Lane Craig has done his homework. He's clearly watched enough of Hitchens's previous debates about religion to know that his opponent shines brightest when propounding his humanistic moral critique of religion—and that Hitchens often finds ways to change the subject back to that critique even when he's supposed to be debating the existence of God. At the beginning of this debate, Craig politely but firmly explains that he's not going to get sidetracked.

> We're not here tonight to debate the social impact of religion, or Old Testament ethics, or biblical inerrancy. All interesting and important topics, no doubt, but not the subject of tonight's debate, which is the existence of God. Consider then my first contention that there's no good argument that atheism is true. Atheists have tried for centuries to disprove the existence of God but no one's ever been able to come up with a successful argument. So, rather than attack straw men at this point I'll just wait to hear Mr Hitchens present his arguments against God's existence and then I'll respond to them in my next speech. In the meantime let's turn to my second main contention that there are good arguments that theism is true.

Craig has prepared so carefully that he's outlined his central arguments on a program distributed to everyone as they enter the hall. His first argument is just the First Cause (or "Cosmological") Argument beloved by medieval philosophers. If there's no God, why is there something rather than nothing?

Hitchens responds by talking about "the nothing coming toward us," by which he means that astronomers say the Andromeda galaxy will eventually collide with us and wipe out the only part of space where life has ever existed. It's a little ambiguous what Hitchens's larger point is here, and some of what he says about this suggests that he's talking about flaws in the design plan allegedly laid down by an all-knowing and infallible designer. That's a legitimate point—but not one that has anything to do with the First Cause Argument.

There *is* a standard atheist response to that argument, or

at least to the simplest version of it. If the reason something can't come from nothing is that nothing can exist without being caused to exist, explaining the existence of the universe by postulating the existence of God just pushes back the question. What caused God to exist? The premise that nothing can exist without a cause not only doesn't get us to the conclusion that God is the First Cause of everything, it gets us to the conclusion that there can't *be* a First Cause, since a First Cause would by definition be an uncaused cause.

Craig is well-aware of this problem. His preferred form of the First Cause Argument, in this debate and in the rest of his work, is the one derived from the Kalām school of medieval Islamic philosophy. This version of the argument starts from the premise not that everything that *exists* has a cause but that everything that *begins* to exist has a cause.

When I talk about the Kalām argument with students in my Introduction to Philosophy classes, I always tell them that this is a fairly plausible-sounding metaphysical principle. I'm usually holding up a cup of coffee in one hand while I'm teaching, and I tell them that if an identical cup of coffee instantaneously came into existence in my other hand, they would be surprised. (No one has ever denied this.) If they asked me what had happened, and I said that "sometimes things just start to exist for no reason," no one would accept this explanation.

So far, so good. But to get from the premise that "everything that begins to exist has a cause of its existence" to the conclusion that "the material universe as a whole has a cause of its existence," never mind the further conclusion that this cause is the deity worshiped by William Lane Craig, we need the assumption that the material universe as a whole hasn't always existed. Why should we assume that?

Craig has two answers. One is an appeal to astrophysics, but—although Craig himself doesn't concede this—that only gets him so far. Even if we accept that all the matter that currently exists can be traced back to a Big Bang thirteen billion years ago, this leaves open the question of whether "our" Bang was the only Bang or just one in a multitude of Big Bangs and Big Crunches whereby some universe expands out of a zero-dimensional space-time point for many billions of years until it eventually starts to contract and ultimately return to such a zero-dimensional singularity. There are string theorists who postulate that our expanding-and-then-dying "soap bubble" of a universe co-exists with a great many other "soap bubbles," with every black hole in our universe becoming the Big Bang of a "baby universe." Neither Craig nor I are particularly qualified to pronounce on scientific debates about theories like this one, and even as I write this paragraph I'm not entirely confident that I've summarized what the physicists are saying accurately, but I do know that even in 2009 the scientific debate has become vastly more complicated than the false dichotomy Craig presents between our universe having always existed and "our" Big Bang being the beginning of *all* material reality.

His second and more interesting move, the one he borrows from the medieval Islamic scholars, is to argue that the universe must have come into existence at a specific point in the past because *nothing* can exist an infinite amount of time. "Infinity," Craig thinks, is a mathematical abstraction that doesn't map onto the real world.

Any atheist with their wits about them here should respond that the "what caused God?" problem reasserts itself at this point in the argument. Did God begin to exist? If so, doesn't He need a cause—and if not, doesn't that mean that He's existed for an infinite amount of time?

Hitchens doesn't think to make this move, but if he had, Craig would have had a response ready. In his many writings on the First Cause Argument, Craig always says that God has existed for neither a finite nor an infinite amount of time because God's existence apart from the existence of the created world isn't "in time." Sometimes, he slips up and says that God's existence "before" the creation of the universe is timeless, but he tries to avoid this formulation for obvious reasons. (St Augustine had similar ideas about the relationship between God and time and ran into similar problems. In what may be the only particularly funny line in his *Confessions*, Augustine says that people sometimes ask him what God's existence was like before the creation of time, and that he tells them that He occupied Himself creating hells for people who ask that question.) Putting the question of whether it's possible to make sense of the idea of a being existing "outside" of time but also creating the universe at a particular moment in time, the better response to Craig here is probably to ask *why* it's supposedly impossible for infinite quantities of time (or anything else) to exist in the real world.

In the debate with Hitchens, he justifies this move with a slightly unclear example about subtracting infinity from infinity. In other work, like a book of battling back-and-forth essays called *Theism, Atheism and Big Bang Cosmology* that Craig wrote with my graduate school professor Quentin Smith, he brings up alleged "paradoxes" about infinite libraries and infinite hotels. Start with the infinite library. To make this easier to visualize, imagine that all the covers of all the books in this library are either red or black and that they alternate—red book, black book, red book, black book—throughout the infinite shelves. Well, Craig asks, when we check a red book out of the infinite library, how many books does that leave? Infinity. In fact, if we check out every one of the infinity of red books out of the infinite library, that still leaves an infinity of black books.

That's pretty strange. The idea that you could check every other book out of a library, so that between each remaining book and the next book on the shelf there's a blank space, and not lower the overall number of books in the process definitely violates our intuitions about how libraries (and indeed quantities of any kind) should work. The infinite hotel example, which Craig takes from the mathematician David Hilbert, is a lot stranger.

Imagine a hotel with an infinite number of rooms and infinite number of guests. Every single room is occupied. Now imagine a new guest wandering into the lobby and asking the night clerk if there are any vacancies. The clerk can say, "No—but I can still give you a room." He simply moves the guest in Room 1 into Room 2, the guest in Room 2 into Room 3, the guest in Room 300,000,000 into Room 300,000,001, and so on into infinity. And if what you're imagining is an infinitely long string of events where each guest is kicked out of her room and then kicks out the person in the next room, you haven't fully wrapped your mind around the counter-intuitiveness of this case. If the night clerk had an infinite PA system that could pipe his voice into all the rooms at once, he could tell everyone what to do, and within fifteen minutes the whole process could be over and done with. Everyone would be bedded down in the room they were going to sleep in that night. No one would have to share a room, no one would have to sleep outside, and there would be a new guest in the mix—*even though every room was occupied at the beginning of the thought experiment.*

This is deeply, deeply weird. Craig takes the weirdness as a sufficient reason to conclude that however useful mathematicians might find the abstract notion of "infinity," it's metaphysically impossible for there to be an infinite quantity of anything in the real world. A philosophically better-trained version of Hitchens might have questioned this inference. Our brains evolved to deal with the sort of things—what the philosopher WVO Quine called "mid-sized dry goods" like cats, dogs, tables, chairs, mountains, galaxies, and so on—that are only ever going to present themselves to us in finite quantities. It's no surprise that our intuitions start going haywire when we start thinking about *infinite* quantities. But why should we think the limits of our puny monkey brains map onto the limits of what's objectively possible? If God exists, His properties are supposed to be pretty difficult for human minds to grasp, too.

A version of Hitchens who knew more about academic debates about the philosophy of religion also would have pushed back in a much clearer way against Craig's extremely dubious opening claim that atheists have never been able to come up with a good argument that there is no God. A standard point theistic philosophers have had to grapple with since at least Epicurus, who wrote about it well over two centuries before the birth of Christ, is that if, as theists often claim, God is definitionally both all-powerful and morally perfect, it's hard to explain why innocents suffer. Wouldn't an all-powerful God be *able* to prevent war, poverty, natural disasters, genocide, and so on? Wouldn't a morally perfect God *want* to do so? Quentin Smith has a paper where he points out that the natural laws dictating that some animals can only survive by killing and eating other animals in savage and painful ways should be added to this list—a particularly awkward example because it has nothing whatsoever to do with human free will and very little to do with any moral lesson that suffering is supposed to impart to any beings capable of reasoning or moral improvement.

Craig and his fellow theists have a number of responses to the atheist's Argument from Evil, but it's at least not blindingly obvious that any of these responses are fully satisfying. Nearly all of them take the form of claiming that some sort of greater good can only be brought about by allowing all of this suffering to occur is *so good* that a morally perfect being would rather have that good and the suffering needed to bring it about than neither one. There's a general structural problem with that move. Beings of limited power like us often have to act indirectly. We bring about X in order to bring about Y because we can't just bring about Y directly. You take a shot that makes you sick for a day in order to make yourself immune from a virus that might make you severely ill or even kill you, and this makes sense because you can't just command yourself to be immune from the virus. A being of unlimited power, though, *can* directly will any Y into being.

Some contemporary theists don't claim to have a *particular* greater good in mind that would fit the bill of somehow being impossible even for an all-powerful being to bring about without allowing innocents to suffer in the process. Still, they insist, there must be *some* solution to this problem. Imagine that an intergalactic spaceship crashes in the street in front of your apartment. You go out and look at the wreckage. You know that the bits and pieces of mysterious machinery you're looking at must have played *some* role in enabling the ship to travel such great distances in such a short period of time. That doesn't mean you're in any position to hazard a specific guess about that role.

Contemporary philosophers call this position "skeptical theism," but it has a long history. It's more or less the answer the voice from the whirlwind gave Job in the Old Testament. I'll leave the question of how satisfying an answer it might be to the judgment of the reader and just note that in this debate Hitchens put up enough of a fight for the issue to come up.

Hitch just dodges the First Cause Argument. He does a bit better—but only a bit—with Craig's version of the Argument from Design, Craig's Douglas Wilson-style appeal to the idea that atheists can't make sense of the idea of objective morality, and Craig's historical argument from the alleged empirical value of the testimony of the authors of the New Testament that they witnessed miracles. He strays more than once into exactly the subjects that Craig rightly said would be off topic in a debate about the existence of God.

Things get really embarrassing in the open discussion part of the debate when Craig tries to figure out whether Hitchens is even really an atheist in the precise sense of that term. Hitchens is certainly a nonbeliever of some sort or another, but atheism isn't the only form of non-belief. Some people define atheism as the absence of a belief in God, which would make agnosticism a type of atheism, but this definition has some pretty odd consequences—for example, it entails that my miniature schnauzer Lucy and my cat Shabazz are "atheists." A clearer way to divide up the concepts is to say that the atheist believes that there isn't a God and the agnostic is someone who's made a decision to reserve judgment. (Some people define agnosticism as *uncertainty* about whether there's a God, but it's surely possible to be a theist, an atheist, or anything else without being one hundred percent sure that your position is correct.) A third non-theistic option, besides atheism and agnosticism, is the old school logical positivist view that sentences like "there is a God" or for that matter "there is not a God" are just *meaningless*—like white noise, or at best like wordless music—because there's no way to verify or falsify them. Craig tries to explain the differences between these three positions, but Hitchens seems to want to endorse *all* of them. This time he's the one who's out of his depth.

VIII. Hitchens vs. Hitchens in Grand Rapids: "Does God exist and is He great?" (2008)

The question is oddly formulated. If God doesn't exist, surely the question of his greatness doesn't come up. To steal an old example batted around in debates about the philosophy of language, it would be like asking a Frenchman in 2008 whether the present King of France is bald. Peter and Christopher both seem to take the separate part of the question as a way of asking whether belief in God is good for humanity.

Christopher's opening presentation is one of the stronger iterations of his humanistic case against religion—although there's a rhetorical trick at the beginning. He starts out with a laugh line about how he doesn't think he'll need a full ten minutes to disprove the existence of God. It's the kind of line that's a little shocking (and thus a little exciting) even to nonbelievers who grew up in religious households. As soon as he's said that, though, he starts to elegantly evade the whole first half of the topic. First, he declines the task of even trying to do what he said it wouldn't take him ten minutes to do, and he redirects the argument to a problem the believer has, not just with proving the existence of God, but also with proving the existence of the specific God of his or her specific religion.

> The atheist proposition is the following—most of the time. It may not be said that there is no God. It may be said that there is no reason to think that there is one. That was the situation after Lucretius and Democritus and the original antitheistic thinkers began their critique of religion, and I would just ask you all, ladies and gentleman, to bear in mind a mild distinction while we go on. You may wish to be a deist, as my heroes Thomas Jefferson and Thomas Paine were, and you may not wish to abandon the idea that there must be *some* sort of first or proximate cause or prime mover of the known and observable world and universe, but even if you can get yourself to that position, which we unbelievers maintain is always subject to better and more perfect and more elegant explanations—even if you can get yourself to that position, all your work is still ahead of you.

So far, his tone has been measured. You get the sense that he's going slow, trying to make sure he arranges the distinction in exactly the right way. In the next part, though, you can see him start to warm to the topic. It's like the bridge in the middle of a song where the tempo starts to change.

> To go from being a deist to a theist, in other words [to become] someone who says God cares about you, knows who you are, minds what you do, cares which bits of your penis or clitoris

you saw away or have sawn away for you, minds who you go to bed with and in what way, minds what holy days you observe, minds what you eat, minds what positions you use for pleasure, all your work is still ahead of you and *lots of luck.*

After a little more talk about the impossibility of moving "from the first position to the second one," and how much trouble he says that even Thomas Aquinas had with it, he says that he "could" and is "strongly tempted" to "leave it there." Rhetorically, this is a good move—if nothing else, he's projecting off-the-charts levels of confidence—but I'm certain that he isn't actually the least little bit tempted, because everything he's said so far is preliminary to what he really wants to talk about, which is his *moral* critique of theistic belief.

[It] is not in my nature to let off a captive audience so easily, so I'll add a couple of things. The reasons why I am *glad* that this is not true would, I suppose, be the gravamen of my case. Some people I know, who are atheists, say they wish they could believe it. Some people I know who are former believers say that they wish they could have their old faith back. They miss it. I don't understand this at all. I think it's an excellent thing that there's no reason to believe in the absurd propositions that I just, admittedly rather briefly, rehearsed to you. The main reason for this, I think, is that it is a totalitarian belief. It is the wish to be a slave.

This is the desire, he says "that there be an unalterable, unchallengeable tyrannical authority" who subjects you "to a total surveillance, around the clock, every waking and sleeping minute of your life" until "the real fun begins" after you're dead. What's being described is a "celestial North Korea." Why would you want this to be true? "Who but a slave desires such a ghastly fate?"

He talks a bit about his travels to North Korea and the eerie parallels between the political system of North Korea and trinitarian Christian doctrine. (The Dear Leader is officially only the head of the Army and head of the Party. The nominal head of state is his dead father Kim Il Sung.) Finally, he points out a limit to the "celestial North Korea" metaphor. The loving Ruler of the Universe postulated by doctrinally standard Christian doctrine continues to rule over you and if you displease him, he will continue to torment you for all eternity after your body dies. This takes him to the most memorable line of the evening. "At least you can fucking *die* and leave North Korea."

He goes on to deride the idea that we need moral guidance from a deity as an insult to our "innate human solidarity." He says that he's so fascinated with religion because it was our first attempt as a species to figure out the nature of the world around us and how we should act in it—"but because it is our first it is our worst." He ends with a recitation of "what you have to believe" to continue to accept any of the monotheistic Western religions in the twenty-first century.

[W]e know things we didn't used to know. We know that the human species...could be as much as two hundred thousand years ago that it becomes separate from the Cro-Magnons and [other hominids]. It could be as little as a hundred. Richard Dawkins thinks two hundred thousand. Francis Collins, who did the Human Genome Project, who's by the way a C.S. Lewis kind of Christian, thinks a hundred thousand. Alright. I'll take a hundred. I'll take a hundred. Here's what you have to believe. For a hundred thousand years, humans are born...[with an] expectation of life...what...twenty-five years for the first few tens of thousands of years?

He paints a vivid picture of what life would have been like

for the vast majority of the time humans existed—the diseases killing people with no apparent explanation, the rampant infant mortality, the violence. "Heaven watches this with folded arms" for ninety-five or ninety-six years, and then "three to four thousand years ago, but only in really barbaric, illiterate parts of the Middle East, not in China...where people can read, or think or do science," the Lord finally decided that He couldn't let this go on. It was time to intervene and reveal His will to His creation.

A common criticism of Hitchens's critique of Christianity (and a common parallel criticism of his critique of other religions with similar beliefs) is that it only applies to "fundamentalist" or "literalist" versions of the faith. I'm sure this is true of at least some of his criticisms, but are the claims that God (a) is all-knowing and (b) rewards and punishes us after we die for what He observes us doing in this life really only part of "fundamentalist" or "literalist" versions of Christian doctrine? Those are the only claims a version of Christianity needs to include in order to be vulnerable to his North Korea analogy, and it seems to be that even an awful lot of Christians prepared to make their peace with the age of the universe theory of evolution, and indeed to ordain women and sanctify same-sex marriages, still accept both (a) and (b) as a matter of course. Similar considerations go for the claim that (c) God's interaction with ancient Israelites (and, then, depending on your flavor of monotheism, subsequent developments) represented an intervention aimed at morally and spiritually improving human beings in a way that hadn't been done before. On that last point, in fact, Hitchens's criticism only applies to versions of the monotheisms that *reject* literalism about a six-day creation.

I won't say that theologically ultra-liberal versions of Christianity that drop all three of these claims don't count as "real" Christianity—or that the parallel versions of other religions that drop them aren't "real" versions of Judaism or Islam—because, again, I agree with Michael Brooks that looking for the "essence" of vast and sprawling traditions is a fool's errand. Even apart from that point, there's something unspeakably silly about an atheist like me passing down rulings about what is the One True Version of any religion. But. These are deep moral criticisms of what are at the very least some *extremely popular* historical and contemporary religious doctrines. They resonated with me when I first watched the stand-alone clip of Hitchens's presentation and I'm still inclined to think that they represent the most compelling part of his case against religion.

In between the debate at Conway Hall and this event in Grand Rapids, the brothers had a falling out over Peter's public recounting of things Christopher supposedly said to him as a young radical. The he-said/he-said gets pretty tangled here, but Peter had recalled Christopher saying *something like* that he wouldn't care if the Red Army was watering its horses in the Thames. Christopher insists that he never said that. He took it as Peter smearing him by portraying him as having been a Stalinist, but that's not the only way to read it. It could have been young Christopher's exaggerated and jokey way of saying that he didn't care who was ahead in the Cold War competition between the great powers because he didn't side with either of them. *Neither Washington nor Moscow but international socialism.*

In any case, after the birth of Peter's third child, the brothers reconciled. Hearing the bitterness in Peter's voice when he mounts the podium, though, you wouldn't know it.

Well, I can tell you're all enjoying the post-Saddam era, which we were told was so good. I wonder whether the invasion of the celestial regions might not be in order—and then we could have a post-God era, which would be of similar delightful quality.

This is actually the second of two back-to-back debates between Christopher and Peter that night in Grand Rapids. The first is painful to watch.

IX.   Hitchens vs. Hitchens in Grand Rapids: "The Iraq War" (2008)

Peter Hitchens is probably a lot more "paleo" a conservative than most of the people referred to as "paleocons." As far as I can tell, his argument for religious faith is that humans are incapable of figuring out whether or not there's a God by the use of our reason, but that we should all make leaps of faith because atheism breeds personal immorality and social disorder. In his book *The Rage Against God*, Peter recalls that the closest thing he had to a religious experience on his journey from being a young Marxist atheist to being whatever he is now happened while gazing at Rogier van der Weyden's fifteenth-century painting *The Last Judgment* during a trip to France when he was in his thirties.

> Still scoffing, I peered at the naked figures fleeing toward the pit of hell, out of my usual faintly morbid interest in the alleged terrors of damnation. But this time I gaped, my mouth [was] actually hanging open. These people did not appear remote or from the ancient past; they were my own generation. Because they were naked, they were not imprisoned in their own age by time-bound fashions. On the contrary, their hair and, in an odd way, the set of their faces were entirely in the style of my own time. They were me and the people I knew. One of them—and I have always wondered how the painter thought of it—is actually vomiting with shock and fear at the sound of the Last Trump.

He's too stylistically conservative an Anglican to let anyone believe that this was *actually* a religious experience. He didn't faint or have a vision or hear voices. He just had a "sudden, strong sense of religion being a thing of the present day, not imprisoned under thick layers of time" and he started to contemplate his various sins.

That's Peter Hitchens. His being Christopher's brother almost feels like something out of a fairy tale where a witch somehow splits various aspects of an individual personality into two separate people. Peter approves of old churches and the old prayerbook and the institution of the monarchy. He disapproves of debauchery and depravity. He worries about creeping socialism.

Above all, Peter Hitchens disapproves of *not taking things seriously*. No one who's familiar with who he is and what he's like should be surprised to hear him say, during his opening presentation during the first of the two debates that night in Grand Rapids, that he was disturbed when he saw a Rear Admiral of the United States Navy addressing his ship's company on television at the beginning of the Iraq War. Their father was in the navy, and Peter's attention is caught by anything naval.

> This was not a stirring or poetic oration. It concluded with the words "it's Hammer Time," and this was succeeded by the playing of a song called, "We Will Rock You." [The audience laughs.] Well yes it is quite funny—except what they then did was launch missiles which then headed toward a country where they would land, inevitably in some cases, on places where entirely innocent people were living.

He goes on to make several arguments about the bad consequences of the war, some of which serve as reminders of how very not radical he is—he worries, for example, that too much money was spent and that the loss of American and British credibility will make it harder to get the public to support other, possibly more necessary, wars in the future. That said, my feeling watching this debate is that the "Hammer Time" moment gets to the core of the issue. The particular form it took may have been shaped by his off-beat hyper-conservative sensibilities, but Peter Hitchens did find his way to a morally appropriate human reaction to the horror of the invasion of Iraq. Christopher, not so much.

## Chapter Five

# What the Hell Happened?

One of my all-time favorite pieces of music on YouTube is a recording of Paul Robeson at a 1949 concert in Moscow. He's singing a Yiddish-language song from the Warsaw Ghetto Uprising, and the combination of the historical backdrop with the cadence of the Yiddish lyrics and Robeson's unmistakable bass baritone makes the experience of listening to it viscerally haunting.

Even so, if I was listening to it in the presence of a Ukrainian or a Chechen, I wouldn't blame them if they told me to turn it off. Robeson was a powerful voice for social equality in the United States as well as, obviously, a supremely talented musician, but he was also an apologist for Joseph Stalin—whose regime was hosting him at that concert.

Stalin deported entire nationalities as a grotesque act of collective punishment. He shipped grain *out of* the Ukraine to sell on the foreign market in the middle of a famine that was killing millions of Ukrainians. He built slave labor camps populated by both actual political dissidents and more than a few people fingered as counterrevolutionaries by neighbors eager to settle petty feuds. Oh, and he let the Warsaw rebels get massacred without lifting a finger to support them—possibly because he was worried about the emergence of an independent power base in post-war Poland.

Robeson didn't know all this in 1949, of course, and some of what we now know about the depth and breadth of Stalin's crimes didn't come out until long afterward. That said, by 1949, Trotskyists and other Soviet dissidents who found their way to the West had been shouting at least some of this stuff from every rooftop that would have them for *decades*. Robeson and other fellow travelers didn't want to listen.

What does all this mean for how I feel about Robeson? His support for Stalin was indefensible on its merits, but if we're interested in evaluating Robeson as a *person* we need to put his enthusiasm for the USSR in the context of his larger politics. He saw its existence as a harbinger of a more egalitarian future and its presence on the world stage as a beacon of hope for oppressed peoples around the world struggling against colonialism and racism. In other words, his view of Stalin's Russia arose out of a genuine desire—however horribly misdirected in this instance—to bring about a better world. That's about the most generous combination of things you can (plausibly) say about Christopher Hitchens's support for the wars in Afghanistan and Iraq.

Left anti-imperialists rightly disgusted by his evolution on these issues often seem to be sure that whatever explains that evolution must be something sad and contemptible. I've talked to people—including one who worked with him at *The Nation*—who told me they thought the excessive drinking just ate his brain. Plenty of others attribute it to Islamophobia arising either from his strident atheism or from plain old jingoism or from both.

There's probably a germ of truth in that one. By his own account, part of Hitchens's reaction to September 11 was a sense of outrage at seeing the country he'd come to think of as his home attacked. And he really did apply some double standards to America and the Middle East. Norman Finkelstein asks a telling question in his essay "On Christopher Hitchens." Given some of the stated justifications for the wars in Afghanistan and Iraq, why didn't Hitch "urge an attack on the United States to capture and punish Henry Kissinger?" Hitchens's response to this point was to say that the United States should punish its own criminals—which isn't exactly an answer.

Even so, the jingoism and Islamophobia explanations only

go so far. The flag lapel pin Hitchens wore during this period wasn't the stars and stripes or the Union Jack. It was the flag of the stateless and overwhelmingly Muslim nation of Kurdistan.

Islamophobia arising from overly intense animosity to religion could conceivably explain Hitchens's support for the war to topple the Taliban in Afghanistan. It's harder to see how any of that explains his support for regime change in Iraq. If anything, it would be a bit easier to see how strident antitheism would lend itself to instinctive suspicion of a grandiose war of "regime change" launched by a born-again Christian who wore his Christianity and his Texan-ness on his sleeve— especially when the regime being changed was a secular one that was brutally effective in suppressing Sunni and Shiite fundamentalists. As I recall, this *was* the attitude of quite a few fans of his at the time who loved watching the religion-bashing "Hitchslap" videos on YouTube but weren't comfortable with his position in Iraq.

The idea that the booze somehow explains anything is even harder to credit. Watch any ninety seconds, selected at random, from any of the Late Hitchens debates covered in the last chapter, and compare them to the checklist of symptoms of alcoholic brain damage. Slowed reaction times? Really? Loss of memory? Please. And the list of Irish revolutionaries and American trade unionists and Canadian prairie socialists who enjoyed whiskey at least as much as Christopher Hitchens did and retained their impeccably leftist convictions until the day they died of liver failure is too long for me to take seriously the idea that bottles of Johnny Walker Black should come with warning labels about how if you drink too much of the stuff you might lose your political bearings and start to support imperialist wars.

What does that leave us with? The most popular explanation by Hitch's angry former comrades is simple opportunism. This is the thesis of the Norman Finkelstein essay.

Finkelstein is, in my view, a mensch. He's suffered real

professional consequences for his advocacy for the Palestinian people. He's entitled to a little disgust with anyone who captured as much of the media limelight as Hitchens did at a time when Hitchens was on the wrong side of a related issue. To the extent that the essay is a raw expression of that disgust, all I can say is, "Fair enough." But as a serious analysis of Hitchens's evolution, it makes very little sense.

Finkelstein's explanation of left "apostates" as a general category is very simple. Apostates are sucked in by "power's magnetic field." The apostate wants to "cash in, or keep cashing in, on earthly pleasures."

A "rite of passage" for apostates is to bash Noam Chomsky. This is the "political equivalent of a bar mitzvah"—a sign that someone has really grown up and become a respectable member of the imperial political community. Oh, and the transition must be complete.

[A]n apostate is usually astute enough to understand that, in order to catch the public eye and reap the attendant benefits, merely registering this or that doubt about one's prior convictions, or nuanced disagreements with former comrades (which, after all, is how a reasoned change of heart would normally evolve), won't suffice. For, incremental change, or fundamental change by accretion, doesn't get the buzz going: there must be a dramatic rupture with one's past.

Finkelstein speculates that Hitchens had been planning his rupture while still mouthing leftist phrases. When he "glimpsed in September 11 the long-awaited opportunity," he realized that "for maximum pyrotechnical effect" he had to completely reverse his politics. If "yesterday he'd called himself a Trotskyist and called Chomsky a comrade," today he was marching arm in arm with George W. Bush and Bush's Assistant Secretary of Defense, Paul Wolfowitz.

The problem with this description is that it doesn't fit *any* of the particulars of this case. Finkelstein describes an abrupt break, but Hitchens had been slowly moving toward an increased willingness to see American military power as a force for good (at least in some contexts) since the mid-1990s. Tellingly, the word "Yugoslavia" doesn't appear in Finkelstein's essay.

Hitch personally spent time in Bosnia in the 90s, and he was strongly motivated by his instinct toward solidarity with that pluralistic multi-ethnic state as it fought for its life against Serbian and sometimes Croatian "ethnic cleansers." He was disturbed by those of his comrades in the Western Left who only seemed to care about the wars in the former Yugoslavia to the extent that they were afraid that the United States would intervene—as, indeed, it ultimately did.

Finkelstein describes "apostates" ritually denouncing Noam Chomsky. Hitchens did no such thing. He continued to pay homage to much of Chomsky's work even as, by the late 90s and especially after 9/11, the two men came to dramatically different conclusions about how to think about a post-Cold War world in which the United States was increasingly coming into conflict not with Communist-led national liberation movements like the Viet Cong but with ugly ethnonationalists like Slobodan Milosevic or mass murdering right-wing dictators like Saddam Hussein.

Chomsky was fiercely opposed to American intervention in Iraq and Yugoslavia. Sending arms to help the Bosnians or later the Kosovars defend themselves might have been one thing, but the Clinton administration's bombing of Serbia in 1999 wasn't far off from Henry Kissinger's infamous instructions during the bombing of Cambodia—"anything that flies on anything that moves." Chomsky and his comrades also had a plausible argument that the effect of this kind of massive-force intervention was actually to accelerate the pace of ethnic cleansing, as militias raced to create "facts on the ground" that would have to be taken into account in an American-imposed peace settlement.

Hitchens didn't see it that way. After years of what he saw as callous American and Western European indifference to the fate of a multi-ethnic republic under siege from Nazi-like forces, he was ready to support just about anything that would save Milosevic's victims. Similarly, and crucially for what came afterward, in the aftermath of the first Gulf War he spent time in the Kurdish region (kept *de facto* autonomous by an American-imposed "no fly zone") in northern Iraq. He was influenced by the pro-war views of local leaders. Some of those leaders had been radical leftists themselves and they knew how to speak Hitch's language. Hitchens had taken a staunchly anti-war position the first time around, but over the course of the 90s he increasingly saw the primary imperative of internationalism as solidarity with the Kurdish enclave. The people he was talking to there saw the United States as a protector and a potential liberator.

There's no doubt in my mind that Chomsky was right and Hitchens was wrong about all of this. As British-Kurdish academic and political analyst Djene Bajalan has pointed out, even if we ignore the tidal wave of human misery the American invasion brought to the *rest* of Iraq, it's hard to see what it did to improve the lives of anyone in the Kurdish area. The end of the economic sanctions certainly helped them, but the United States could have ended those at any time without invading the country. Hell, it could have kept them in place but exempted the Kurdish region. Meanwhile, the chaos unleashed by the invasion unleashed plenty of lethally anti-Kurdish political and religious forces, and the status of Iraqi Kurdistan itself— *de facto* but not *de jure* independent, and not terribly internally democratic—stayed about the same.

That said, the idea that the deepening disagreements Hitchens and Chomsky had over the course of the 90s and

2000s represented the "political equivalent of a bar mitzvah" in which Hitchens proved himself to the powers that be by throwing his old comrade under the bus just doesn't map onto the details of the case. Late Hitchens's consistently expressed view was that Chomsky had done good work in opposing the crimes of Nixon and Kissinger in Indochina and of the Reagan Administration in Central America but that he'd let an overly kneejerk anti-imperialism guide him to positions that no longer made sense in a world where the empire's enemies could hardly have been more different from Ho Chi Minh or the Sandinistas. If anything, Chomsky was far more harshly critical of Hitchens than *vice versa*.

More generally, far from flagellating himself and declaring that he'd seen the light about how wrong he'd been across the board until 9/11, Hitchens's consistent rhetorical strategy was to emphasize the *continuities* between his old and new positions. As un-Trotskyist as his views on American imperialism might now be, he continued to express admiration for Trotsky himself as well as for a laundry list of other dissident Marxists. At the same time, to justify his positions on Yugoslavia, Afghanistan, and Iraq, he tended to lean on rhetorical echoes of the Popular Front Against Fascism promoted by the Stalinist Communist movement in the 1930s.

He also didn't abandon all or even *most* of his positions on other matters after 9/11. He continued to support reparations for slavery. He broke from the pro-war camp on the issues of torture and mass surveillance. And as a militant atheist, his positions on the attention-grabbing culture war issues of the first decade of the twenty-first century aligned him far more with the sensibilities of the anti-war left than those of the evangelicals who dominated the Bush administration.

Most strikingly, Hitchens continued to support the Palestinian cause until the end of his life. In one particularly striking C-SPAN clip, a caller asks how the United States can use the UN resolutions violated by Saddam Hussein as a pretext for war while ignoring all the resolutions violated by Israel. Hitchens agrees that this is hypocritical and warns that America's continued complicity in Israel's "appalling mistreatment" of the Palestinians threatens to undermine international support for the just and necessary war to liberate the people of Iraq from Saddam Hussein.

He moderated his longstanding support for a secular democratic one-state solution to a more pragmatic two-state view, but he had no patience for apologists for Israel's behavior. As that C-SPAN clip continues, fellow guest Andrew Sullivan gets increasingly upset at what he sees as Hitch's willingness to excuse Palestinian terrorism. Hitchens calmly reiterates that the people of Palestine have a right to resist their oppressors. It just doesn't make sense to him to put this resistance in the same moral category as religious fanatics traveling to a distant country to fly planes into buildings.

Here he is on the same subject in *Hitch-22* — a book published, remember, a year before he died.

Suppose that a man leaps out of a burning building — as my dear friend and colleague Jeff Goldberg sat and said to my face over a table at La Tomate in Washington not two years ago — and lands on a bystander in the street below. Now, make the burning building be Europe, and the luckless man underneath be the Palestinian Arabs. Is this a historical injustice? Has the man below been made a victim, with infinite cause of complaint and indefinite justification for violent retaliation? My own reply would be a provisional "no," but only on these conditions. The man leaping from the burning building must still make such restitution as he can to the man who broke his fall, and must not pretend that he never even landed on him. And he must base his case on the singularity and uniqueness of the original leap. It can't, in other words, be "leap, leap, leap" for four generations and more. The people underneath cannot be expected to tolerate leaping on this scale and of this duration, if you catch my drift.

Progressive Except for Palestine (PEP) is an epithet for those on the soft Left who are too emotionally attached to Israel to take a stand against that country's human rights abuses. The foreign policy views of Late Hitchens made him almost the opposite of that—perhaps a NEP (Neocon Except for Palestine) or more accurately a NEPTS (Neocon Except for Palestine, Torture and Surveillance). And while he greatly deemphasized domestic policy in general in this period, to the extent that he did talk about it his positions were progressive.

Let's dispense with the Finkelstein's belief that Hitchens was only claiming to be pro-war to "cash in" and admit that his messy combination of views came from a good faith attempt to muddle his way through a world that was very different from the one in which he joined Peter Sedgwick for that "pint of tepid British beer" in 1966. What *does* explain how Hitch ended up on the wrong side of history?

Tariq Ali half-jokingly suggests in his 2004 book *Bush in Babylon: The Recolonization of Iraq* that Hitchens died in the Twin Towers on 9/11 and "[t]he vile replica currently on offer is a double." But more than a few critics seem to have embraced the opposite explanation. They think the problem with Hitchens was that there was *too much* continuity between his old and his new politics.

These critics fall into two categories. Some radicals think the best way to advance the socialist cause is to act as cheerleaders for every regime that put a red star on its flag. Leftists of this stripe view Trotskyism as a sort of gateway drug that leads its users to gradually abandon socialism altogether and drift into the imperialist camp. This is presumably what George

Galloway was getting at when he included "ex-Trotskyist" in his "popinjay" jab. On the other end, right-wing isolationists who opposed the Iraq War on America First grounds hate Trotskyism because they hate Marxism and revile the memory of the Russian Revolution. Writing in Pat Buchanan's magazine *The American Conservative* in 2005, Tom Piatak calls Hitchens a "lover of Trotsky and hater of God" whose support for wars to expand democracy to the Middle East amounted to a desire to "use American power to bring about a world revolution."

Proto-Trumpists like Piatak and soft neo-Stalinists like Galloway agreed (for very different reasons) that there was an intimate connection between Hitchens's past Trotskyism and his current pro-war position. Members of both groups liked to rattle off a list of historical and contemporary figures who'd found their way from Trotskyism to neoconservatism to try to establish a causal connection between the two. Piatak goes as far as to claim that neoconservatism just *is* "warmed-over Trotskyism."

Sometimes people cheat and try to pad out the list by adding figures like Paul Wolfowitz, whose personal connection to Trotskyism seems to consist of the historian Steven Schwartz having once told the journalist Jeet Heer that he (Schwartz) had once been at a party with Wolfowitz where the two men "exchanged banter" about Trotskyism and related subjects. As far as I can tell, that line in Heer's article about Trotskyism and neoconservatism really is where everyone got the idea that Wolfowitz somehow fell into this category. Schwartz himself, incidentally, is a neoconservative who may be an "ex-Trotskyist," but only because he seems to be an ex-*everything*. The late (actually) Trotskyist writer Louis Proyect once described Schwartz like this:

There is not a single political or religious sect that he has not dipped his big toe in, from Trotskyism, anarchism, and "libertarian socialism" on the left, to Buckleyite conservatism on the right. He is now a devout Sufi Muslim, a faith that he discovered in the Balkans while writing pleas on behalf of imperialist intervention. The old Jewish saying would apply to Schwartz: "A chazer bleibt a chazer." (A pig remains a pig.)

Take the likes of Schwartz and Wolfowitz out of it, though, and I'm sure you can still find a dozen or so figures who spent serious time in the Trotskyist movement and then drifted so far in the other direction that they became neoconservative warmongers. Does this show that something *about Trotskyism* explains that transition?

Some of the most obvious problems with this analysis are: 1-That the overwhelming majority of "neocons" were never Trotskyists, 2-That the overwhelming majority of Trotskyists, even the ones who stopped being Trotskyists, never became neocons, 3-That ex-radicals of one sort or another drifting to the right is a depressingly common phenomenon and has been for so long that for every Irving Kristol who went from Trotskyism to conservatism there's probably a Whittaker Chambers or ten whose starting point was *Stalinism* (or at least post-Stalin mainstream communism), and most of all 4-That Christopher Hitchens himself was at best an extremely ambiguous example of the phenomenon. As we've seen, he agreed with the neocons about Iraq, but he disagreed with them about plenty.

To understand how Hitchens went wrong, we have to look not at where his politics started in 1966, but at what happened to them at the end of the 1990s. As late as the death penalty debate in 1997, Hichens took it for granted that the ultimate horizon of his politics is the creation of a "classless society." Six years later, in his foreword to a new edition of Aldous Huxley's *Brave New World*, he casually clumps together "the search for Utopia or the end of history or the classless society" as undertakings of the same type.

As far as I know, there are only two passages anywhere in his many books where he reflects on his ideological shift. The first, already mentioned at the end of Chapter Three, comes in *Letters to a Young Contrarian*:

> I have not, since you ask, abandoned all the tenets of the Left. I still find that the materialist conception of history has not been surpassed as a means of analyzing matters; I still think that there are opposing class interests; I still think that monopoly capitalism can and should be distinguished from the free market and that it has certain fatal tendencies in both the short and long term. But I have learned a good deal from the libertarian critique of this worldview, and along with this has come a respect for those who upheld that critique when almost all the reigning assumptions were statist.

The second, more reflective and self-effacing, passage comes nine years later in *Hitch-22*:

> Alteration of mind can creep up on you: for a good many years I maintained that I was a socialist if only to distinguish myself from the weak American term "liberal," which I considered evasive. Brian Lamb, the host of C-Span cable television, bears some of the responsibility for this. Having got me to proudly announce my socialism once, on the air, he never again had me as a guest without asking me to reaffirm the statement. It became the moral equivalent of a test of masculinity: I wouldn't give him or his audience the satisfaction of a denial. Then I sat down to write my *Letters to a Young Contrarian*, and made up my mind to address the letters to real students whose faces and names and questions I had to keep in mind. What was I to say when they asked my advice about "commitment"? They all wanted to do

something to better the human condition. Well, was there an authentic socialist movement for them to join, as I would once have said there was? Not really...Could a real internationalist "Left" be expected to revive? It didn't seem probable. I abruptly realized that I had no right to bluff or to bullshit the young. (Late evenings with old comrades retelling tales of old campaigns weren't exactly dishonest, but then they didn't really count, either.) So I didn't so much repudiate a former loyalty, like some attention-grabbing defector, as feel it falling away from me. On some days, this is like the phantom pain of a missing limb. On others, it's more like the sensation of having taken off a needlessly heavy overcoat.

He doesn't mention libertarians in that second passage, which might suggest that the last sentence of the first one was just a matter of an old ideological warrior giving due respect to the veterans on the other side. I certainly know of no passage anywhere in his writings in the ensuing years where he advocates privatizations or cuts to social services or anything else that would indicate that whatever it is that he learned from the libertarian critique had moved him as far as actually adopting any libertarian positions. And in his 2006 book on Thomas Paine he pays tribute to Paine (among many other things) for being a visionary early advocate of something like a welfare state.

That said, you can find a handful of sentences scattered around Hitch's writings in the last decade where he flirts with a surprisingly right-wing diagnosis of the atrocities committed by capital-C Communist regimes in the twentieth century. The anti-Stalinist Marxists whose memory he exults even in *Letters to a Young Contrarian* saw those horrors as a result of the Soviet Union's departure from core socialist ideals. Without social ownership of the *state*—in other words, without democracy—state ownership just means the economic and political domination of a handful of officials over the mass of workers and peasants. The fewer hands power is concentrated in, the more likely that power is to be abused. This basic truth explains the labor practices of Gilded Age robber barons no less than Stalin's purges. The 1986 or even 1997 Hitchens presumably would have signed off on this analysis. In the passages I have in mind, though, he drifts into seeing these horrors as adding up to a cautionary tale about "utopianism," which he equates with human experimentation on a mass scale. He sometimes says that the people killed by such regimes were being disposed of like the "waste product" of "failed experiments."

As good a line as this is, the underlying thought doesn't stand up to scrutiny. Experimenting with *social institutions* to make them less brutal and hierarchical is precisely the opposite of trying to perfect individual human beings. Where reactionaries see individual immorality as the source of social ills, and exhortations to individual reform as the answer, the socialist Left focuses on changing societal structures. This approach is fully compatible with seeing human beings as generally incapable of moral perfection. In fact, the more you suspect that giving one human too much power over others will lead him to treat those others the way Jeff Bezos treats workers in his warehouses, or the way that Harvey Weinstein treated aspiring starlets, the more you should want to distribute power as evenly as possible. That's as good an argument as any for workers' control of the means of production.

It's hard to say whether these anti-utopian passages represented a decisive shift in Hitchens's view of the desirability of socialism. One example that suggests otherwise comes in the post-*Koba* exchange with Martin Amis. He notes that Amis is writing from Uruguay, a country whose "thousand-mile beaches" Amis had written fondly about...and whose regime had an extensive history of torturing and disappearing its citizens. As Hitchens considers this point, he strikes an ambivalent note on the Utopianism Question.

The Uruguayan oligarchy was probably smart in making few claims for itself while it was doing this. It certainly didn't announce that it was trying to bring about a workers' paradise. The mere boast that it was doing it in order to ward off communism was enough to keep the weapons and "advisers" coming from my home town of Washington, DC, and to procure an uncritical silence from most Western "intellectuals."

You scorn the sinister illusion of human perfectibility, as well you may. But—though I don't criticize you for idealizing Uruguay as a counter revolutionary tourist—I do earnestly hint to you that there may yet be more scope for radical human improvement.

My best guess about all of this is that the passage in *Hitch-22* was Hitchens's introspectively honest reflection on the change. He abandoned the socialist cause not because he no longer thought that the "more enlightened application of the idea in the non-capitalist future" he'd talked about in the debate with Biswanger and Ridpath was *desirable* but because it no longer seemed realistically possible that such a future would ever come about. His thoughts about the very idea of radical change sometimes drifted in a more cynical and conservative direction in the following years, but that wasn't the cause of the original break.

This was the most important alteration in Hitchens's politics and, contra Norman Finkelstein, it involved no pyrotechnics whatsoever. Hitch wrote (ahem) God knows how many thousands of pages in his last decade, and you need to have read damn near all of them to even know about the existence of the two passages I quoted earlier. What this probably shows is that, long before he realized that his views had changed, Hitchens had been gradually worn down by the political atmosphere of the 1990s, where every talking head in the world took it for granted that the great struggles between visions of how to organize society that had characterized the twentieth century had ended with the fall of the Soviet Union. In this era, even if you didn't *want* to believe Margaret Thatcher's dictum that "there is no alternative," it was part of the ideological drinking water.

By the time Hitchens's politics shifted, he'd spent much of his life as a globe-trotting journalist getting to know people who lived under despotic regimes. During the decades when his radical Left convictions were intact, he presumably believed that some fresh wave of socialist revolutions would one day sweep those regimes into the dustbin of history. When he gave up on that, he still wasn't ready to give up hope on there being *some* other path to democratic transformation.

In the double header debate with Peter in Grand Rapids, Christopher expresses disgust at the people who would argue with him about the invasion at Washington, DC, cocktail parties, starting their sentences with, "I know Saddam is a bad guy, but..." You could say that the fact that he was at such parties in the first place tells you something, and fair enough, but he'd been going to them for a long, long time, and he still didn't quite belong there. Hitch remained enough of a radical, at least in his fundamental instincts, to be disgusted by this kind of *realpolitik* indifference to brutal oppression. A *bad guy?* During the Q&A after the debate, a questioner with a beard and glasses who looks like he time traveled to the 2008 debate from a 2018 Brooklyn DSA meeting, asks him if he's prepared to admit that America's "adventure in Iraq" is imperial. Hitch's response is that of course it is. The United States was an empire in 1968 when the CIA helped install "the Saddam Hussein wing of the Baath Party" in power. It was an empire in 1994 when Henry Kissinger lied to the Iraqi Kurds, promising US support for an uprising.

That was just as imperial. The United States was an Empire when Jimmy Carter gave the green light to Saddam Hussein to invade Iran in 1980 and told them, with American intelligence supplied by satellite through Saudi Arabia, that they would achieve a swift victory over the Iranians and probably recover the...Arabic-speaking territories of Khuzestan [in] Persia for Iraqi control. That war, we reckon, I've been to the cemeteries in Iran and in Baghdad, that war, probably not less than a million and a half casualties...All of these were imperial.

He follows this up with some sophistry about how if the United States is imperial, *everything it does* is imperial, so it would have been just as imperial not to intervene as to intervene. To see what's wrong with that, compare: if Hannibal Lecter is a murderer, everything he does is murderous. Lecter *not* killing people and eating their livers would be just as murderous as him doing so.

Hitchens being Hitchens, he can do a little better than that. He follows it up with some plausible-sounding points about forces on the "imperialist and conservative Right" (he names Kissinger, Brent Sowcroft, Bush Sr., and "the Saudi lobby, which is the heart of imperialism in my hometown of Washington, DC") which had cynical imperial reasons for wanting to keep Saddam Hussein in power. Fair enough, but if Tony Soprano has cynical, self-interested, gangsterish reasons for deciding not to order a particular hit and he decides to do it anyway, "it would have been just as gangsterish if I hadn't done it" would be half-true but entirely irrelevant as a response to someone pointing out that having your enemies whacked is a despicably gangsterish thing to do.

Putting aside *that* defense, the real core of Hitch's answer comes when, after listing off all the imperial meddling the United States did *on behalf* of Saddam Hussein in the past, he says, "In 2003, for the first time I know about, the United States intervened in Iraq on the right side."

That's the real point. Earlier that night, and in other debates, Hitchens made more pragmatic arguments for the war—all of which, of course, have aged terribly. One was that if Saddam Hussein's regime crumbled on its own instead of being removed by US intervention, Iraq would collapse into a failed state. (Perhaps it would have had years of bloody sectarian civil wars, and ISIS would have arisen there and in Syria, and... and...) Another was it was a great victory for the larger cause of disarmament. Gaddafi turned over his own stockpile of Weapons of Mass Destruction because he didn't want to be next. (Libya was next anyway, and in the aftermath of that war it became even more of a failed state than Iraq.) He also made the legalistic argument that states can give up their sovereignty if they commit a certain checklist of crimes. (As Tom Gorman pointed out in a 2005 article in *CounterPunch* called "The Hitchens Doctrine," the United States had ticked every one of those boxes—as Hitchens of all people should have known.) These are all easy to knock down because they're rationalizations, and pretty thin ones at that.

During the Cold War, Hitchens was a critic of what the Russian Revolution had degenerated into, but he still held out hope for a revival of its original ideals. By 2003, the only revolution that seemed to him to be realistically available for export was the American Revolution. Lacking any other plausible agent of democratic change in the Middle East, he was willing at last to turn to what he knew damn well was still an empire.

That Hitchens wanted to base his politics on solidarity with oppressed people is admirable. That he closed his eyes to the profound difference between some despot being overthrown in a popular revolution and the same despot being deposed by an occupying army that would inevitably be bitterly resented by most of the population of the conquered country is not.

The waste products of failed imperial experiments tend to involve depleted uranium and grandmothers watching their grandchildren ripped apart by cluster bombs.

Late Hitchens's belief that the United States military could be the vehicle for exporting democratic revolution if only it were pointed in the right directions was, at best, a tragic mistake. The "Trotskyism leads to neoconservatism" diagnosis, though, gets the nature of that mistake exactly wrong.

Trotskyism is a flavor of socialist thought that comes with plenty of flaws. Trotskyists are often dogmatic and purist. They have a bad habit of splintering into increasingly tiny sects based on esoteric disagreements. American Trotskyists, in my experience, have a bad habit of deriving ideas about political strategy more from reading the writings of long-dead revolutionaries than from a realistic analysis of contemporary American conditions.

At its best, though, the Trotskyist tradition represented a principled and valuable refusal to choose between atrocities. Rather than acting as apologists for either the empire napalming peasants in Vietnam or the Eastern European police states that wrapped themselves in the red flag while crushing anyone who so much as tried to organize a real labor union, Trotskyists held out hope for that "more enlightened application" of socialist ideals he talked about in 1986.

The problem with Hitchens in the final phase of his career isn't that there was too much residual Trotskyism in his political bloodstream. It's that there was far too little.

## Chapter Six

# Remembering Christopher Hitchens

Christopher Hitchens died on December 15, 2011. The next morning, I'd planned to give my friend Ryan Lake a ride to the airport. When I stopped by his apartment to pick him up, he poured us two glasses of Johnny Walker Black. Neither of us was or is in the habit of drinking before noon, but it was the last time we were going to be seeing each other for a few weeks and we both wanted to toast Hitch. I did the same thing with my brother David when I saw him a few days later.

Eight years before, I'd been deeply involved in organizing anti-war protests in my hometown of Lansing, Michigan. Later, when I went to the University of Miami to pursue a Ph.D., I became far less politically active. I had the same socialist and anti-imperialist theoretical commitments I'd always had, but my political involvement was pretty much limited to reading Glenn Greenwald columns about drones and civil liberties at *Salon* and using them as cheat sheets when I was out at the bar with my liberal friends and we started arguing about Obama and drones.

I'd been reading Hitchens on and off since high school and I'd been deeply disappointed by the drift of his post-9/11 politics. Ryan shares every ounce of my anti-war commitments. So does my brother. So why did we continue to admire him enough that it went without saying that we'd hoist glasses of Johnny Walker in his honor when he died?

In my case, at least, it's not always easy to disentangle the reasons. Politics have become central to my life again in the years since I finished grad school—more so than ever before, in some ways. I host a show called GTAA (Give Them An Argument). DSA branches sometimes invite me to come speak to them. I've somehow even made it onto the masthead of my favorite political magazine, *Jacobin*, as a columnist. Even so, one part of the enduring appeal of Hitchens for me comes from my lifelong interest in the non-political parts of philosophy.

I spend a lot of my life these days in a world of left-wing writers and YouTube commentators where many people claim to be bored by the metaphysical forever war between atheism and religion. Sure, the attitude seems to be, it's fine to have gone through a New Atheist phase in 2009, and even to feel some nostalgia for the days when you could get excited about the subject, but surely now we can all see that continuing to be interested in that stuff is "cringe."

Counterpoint: All human beings die. We all mourn the deaths of people we love. We all at least *tell ourselves* that we're trying to be good people while we're here. Are you bored yet?

Well, some people insist that death isn't the end of human existence. The all-powerful creator of the universe has preserved the minds of your loved ones and will preserve your mind, when it's your time to go, in some sort of eternal state of reward and punishment. More than a few believers go so far as to add that if you're skeptical about all of this you can't be a good person, or perhaps you won't be able to make sense of what moral goodness *is*, or even if you can it's very unlikely that you'll be *motivated* to be truly good.

I guess some people who profess to be bored by the whole subject are atheists so comfortable in their non-belief that they think of these claims the way the rest of us think of the various propositions being propounded by the homeless woman who stands on the street corner screaming about the microchip the aliens put in her nostril—even though atheistic materialism is the metaphysical position of a distinct minority of the human race. All I can say is that, speaking purely for myself, I do still find the subject pretty interesting.

One of Hitchens's least useful legacies was the contribution he made to the formation of contemporary Atheism with a capital A—to the idea of atheism not just as a philosophical position but as a political "movement." That part never made sense to me. I don't object to people who have rejected religion coming together to discuss this common interest, any more than I object to people coming together to share their love of birding or mountain-climbing, but what would an Atheist Movement be a movement *for*?

It's true that there are issues, like abortion rights and the separation of church and state, where atheists are more likely to be on the right side than people with other beliefs, but plenty of progressive Christians, hippie Western Buddhists, and so on are also on that side. I would think the most effective movements on these issues aren't ones that are divided along the basis of participants' metaphysical beliefs. Conversely, some of the people who get excited about Atheism as a Movement don't share very many of my political goals. They're libertarians whose policy prescriptions would lead to an unregulated market for desperate people to sell their own organs to scrape together enough bitcoin to feed their families. Or they're neocons who think that secular liberalism should be brought to the people of Iran by the 82nd Airborne. Or worse.

That said, you don't have to be an Atheist with a capital A to be interested in thinking hard about the subjects Christopher Hitchens spent so much of the last period of his life debating. He couldn't go toe to toe on the Kalām Cosmological Argument with William Lane Craig, just as I suspect that he couldn't have gone toe to toe with G.A. Cohen on Marxism after he'd gotten to the point when the best he could do on that subject was to mumble in *Letters to a Young Contrarian* that he held out hope for somehow prying apart "monopoly capitalism" from "the free market," but that doesn't stop me from thinking that his humanistic moral critique of the Abrahamic religions was interesting and that at least some parts of it were compelling.

He also wrote so much about figures like T.S. Eliot and Jane Austen and Marcel Proust and F. Scott Fitzgerald that a book like this one could have been written just on Hitch as a literary critic. In fact, I hope that someone does write that book. It couldn't be me, though. I've read about five percent of his source material. Honestly, the part of Hitchens's output that's most important to me has always been the part that became the most indefensible in the last part of his life—his political commentary.

It's tempting to imagine a timeline where Hitchens beat the cancer and found his way back to the best version of his politics. Reading the passage in *Hitch-22* about how he didn't feel like it was likely that there would ever be a revived "authentic socialist movement" for his students at the New School to join, it's tempting to imagine a version of Hitchens who continued in his teaching position there until he started to interact with the kind of young people who read *Jacobin* and knocked on doors for Bernie. Who knows where *that* would have led him?

The problem with this fantasy is that his pro-war stance in the 2000s estranged him from so many of his former comrades that it might not be psychologically realistic to think he could have admitted to himself that he'd been wrong and all the people who denounced him at the time had been right. Most likely, any grudging support he gave to the resurgent Left would have been *despite* the young socialists' deep opposition to America's wars in the Middle East. It's particularly hard to imagine him having anything kind to say about one of the most important figures in the global revival of the socialist Left—peacenik British Labour leader Jeremy Corbyn.

I can also imagine a version of Hitchens so infuriated by the presidency of Donald Trump that he became a particularly insufferable sort of MSNBC liberal. It's easy to imagine him reacting to the spectacle of a crowd of cranks and racists and conspiracy theorists storming the Capitol on January 6 the way he reacted to 9/11—an event that he described as the beginning of "a war to the finish between everything I love and everything I hate." Or we could have seen a version of Hitch who became steadily more interested in the kind of edgy cultural commentary that many people who liked his earlier work would have just found embarrassing. This is a man, after all, who once wrote an essay called "Why Women Aren't Funny."

Regardless of which Hitch we ended up with, I suspect that if the cancer had gone into remission for a decade and he'd died yesterday, I would have ended up having the same mixed feelings about him that I had in 2011. I hated parts of his work and loved most of the rest. He was always worth reading and watching and he was always worth thinking about and arguing with in your head. That's very far from being a nothing.

Christopher Hitchens spent years writing for *Slate*. Can you remember reading anything at *Slate* in 2019 or 2020 or 2021 that made you think? How about *Salon*? How about *The Daily Beast*? Can you remember anything you read in any of these places that made you grumble "damn, that's actually really good" even though you disagreed with the author's conclusion? Hell, can you remember a single turn of phrase from anything you read in any of these places more than a week ago?

The veil separating longform articles from social media posts feels a little thinner every day. Whether I'm reading 3000 words on why *The Muppet Show* was, in retrospect, *extremely problematic* or 5000 words on why people who think *The Muppet Show* was problematic *are as bad as the East German secret police*, I can't help but think that we need more Christopher Hitchenses. I'd like for the new ones to be more like the Hitchens of 1986 or 1997 or even 1999 than the Hitchens of 2002, but when I think about his response to Martin Amis in *Slate* that year, I desperately want even that Hitchens back. Really, things have gotten bad enough that one won't be enough. We need a hundred of him.

# Acknowledgments

I should start as always with the many debts of gratitude I owe to my beautiful wife, Jennifer, who does things like ask, "Are you working right now?" when I'm on Twitter. I can't imagine actually finishing a book without her.

I wouldn't have *started* this one without Michael Brooks, but let's hold that thought for now.

Ed and Diane Buckner took the time to proofread the manuscript before I turned it in. There's absolutely no reason why they should have volunteered to take on that task except that they're ridiculously excellent people.

Josh Strawn studied with both Slavoj Žižek and Christopher Hitchens at the New School. In a Zoom discussion when I was first starting to write this book, he told me that he'd tried to arrange a debate between the two giants on the subject of the Iraq War. Both were up for it, but the schedules never quite worked out. As well as sharing his stories, Josh helped to shape my analysis in Chapter Six of how Hitch's politics might have shifted if he'd survived.

In 2008, my friend Mark Warren dressed as "vampire Christopher Hitchens" for Halloween. The costume consisted of plastic vampire fangs, a sports jacket, and a glass of whiskey that never left his hand. That memory made me laugh enough times while I was writing this to merit a shoutout here.

I've had too many interesting and valuable Hitchens conversations with too many people to name them all, but two that were important enough that it would feel ungrateful not to mention them here are the ones I had with *Jacobin* editor Bhaskar Sunkara and *People's Republic of Walmart* co-author Leigh Philipps.

In a very different way, I suppose I should thank Pastor Douglas Wilson. He's an unsavory character in multiple ways—

it takes about ten seconds on Google, for example, to find some pretty astonishing quotes from him on the subject of "the war between the states"—but I can't imagine a better way to prepare to write about his polemics against Christopher Hitchens on atheism and the foundations of morality than by having my own debate with him on the topic. He was a good sport.

During the final year of Michael Brooks's life, I did a weekly segment on his podcast and YouTube show TMBS (The Michael Brooks Show) called The Debunk. In the last months, we'd sometimes mix it up and follow up that segment with a "throwback clip" from ten or twenty years ago. In one of the many text messages that I've spent far too much time staring at during the last year, he asks if I want to do a throwback clip on that night's show and he suggests that the untold hours of Hitch on YouTube are always a fun well to draw from for such clips. The idea for this book grew out of those TMBS segments and Michael encouraged me to write it. I signed the contract with Zero Books ten days before he died.

The fact that he's not around to read these pages makes me feel ill. It's been more than a year and I still feel the itch to shoot him a text message at least once a week. Finished the Hitchens book? I should text Michael. Re-watched a particularly good *Sopranos* episode? I should text Michael. He was deeply interested in Buddhist spirituality. He went to silent meditation retreats. He certainly seemed to believe that some immaterial aspect of him would persist after he died. It was one of the only subjects on which we really disagreed. We never exactly argued about it—but he would tease me in an indirect way about my lack of openness to ideas that went beyond my materialist assumptions about the universe.

Whatever the truth might turn out to be about what happens when we die, I'll do everything I can while I'm here to make sure Michael's *memory* stays alive.

# CULTURE, SOCIETY & POLITICS

The modern world is at an impasse. Disasters scroll across our smartphone screens and we're invited to like, follow or upvote, but critical thinking is harder and harder to find. Rather than connecting us in common struggle and debate, the internet has sped up and deepened a long-standing process of alienation and atomization. Zer0 Books wants to work against this trend. With critical theory as our jumping off point, we aim to publish books that make our readers uncomfortable. We want to move beyond received opinions.

Zer0 Books is on the left and wants to reinvent the left. We are sick of the injustice, the suffering and the stupidity that defines both our political and cultural world, and we aim to find a new foundation for a new struggle.

If this book has helped you to clarify an idea, solve a problem or extend your knowledge, you may want to check out our online content as well. Look for Zer0 Books: Advancing Conversations in the iTunes directory and for our Zer0 Books YouTube channel.

## Popular videos include:

*Žižek and the Double Blackmain*

*The Intellectual Dark Web is a Bad Sign*

*Can there be an Anti-SJW Left?*

*Answering Jordan Peterson on Marxism*

Follow us on Facebook
at https://www.facebook.com/ZeroBooks  and Twitter at https://twitter.com/Zer0Books

## Bestsellers from Zer0 Books include:

**Give Them An Argument**
Logic for the Left
Ben Burgis
Many serious leftists have learned to distrust talk of logic. This is a serious mistake.
Paperback: 978-1-78904-210-8 ebook: 978-1-78904-211-5

**Poor but Sexy**
Culture Clashes in Europe East and West
Agata Pyzik
How the East stayed East and the West stayed West.
Paperback: 978-1-78099-394-2 ebook: 978-1-78099-395-9

**An Anthropology of Nothing in Particular**
Martin Demant Frederiksen
A journey into the social lives of meaninglessness.
Paperback: 978-1-78535-699-5 ebook: 978-1-78535-700-8

**In the Dust of This Planet**
Horror of Philosophy vol. 1
Eugene Thacker
In the first of a series of three books on the Horror of Philosophy,
*In the Dust of This Planet* offers the genre of horror as a way of
thinking about the unthinkable.
Paperback: 978-1-84694-676-9 ebook: 978-1-78099-010-1

**The End of Oulipo?**
An Attempt to Exhaust a Movement
Lauren Elkin, Veronica Esposito
Paperback: 978-1-78099-655-4 ebook: 978-1-78099-656-1

**Capitalist Realism**
Is There No Alternative?
Mark Fisher
An analysis of the ways in which capitalism has presented itself
as the only realistic political-economic system.
Paperback: 978-1-84694-317-1 ebook: 978-1-78099-734-6

**Rebel Rebel**
Chris O'Leary
David Bowie: every single song. Everything you want to know,
everything you didn't know.
Paperback: 978-1-78099-244-0 ebook: 978-1-78099-713-1

**Kill All Normies**
Angela Nagle
Online culture wars from 4chan and Tumblr to Trump.
Paperback: 978-1-78535-543-1 ebook: 978-1-78535-544-8

## Cartographies of the Absolute
Alberto Toscano, Jeff Kinkle
An aesthetics of the economy for the twenty-first century.
Paperback: 978-1-78099-275-4 ebook: 978-1-78279-973-3

## Malign Velocities
Accelerationism and Capitalism
Benjamin Noys
Long listed for the Bread and Roses Prize 2015, *Malign Velocities*
argues against the need for speed, tracking acceleration
as the symptom of the ongoing crises of capitalism.
Paperback: 978-1-78279-300-7 ebook: 978-1-78279-299-4

## Meat Market
Female Flesh under Capitalism
Laurie Penny
A feminist dissection of women's bodies as the fleshy fulcrum of
capitalist cannibalism, whereby women are both consumers and
consumed.
Paperback: 978-1-84694-521-2 ebook: 978-1-84694-782-7

## Babbling Corpse
Vaporwave and the Commodification of Ghosts
Grafton Tanner
Paperback: 978-1-78279-759-3 ebook: 978-1-78279-760-9

## New Work New Culture
Work we want and a culture that strengthens us
Frithjof Bergmann
A serious alternative for mankind and the planet.
Paperback: 978-1-78904-064-7 ebook: 978-1-78904-065-4

**Romeo and Juliet in Palestine**
Teaching Under Occupation
Tom Sperlinger
Life in the West Bank, the nature of pedagogy and the role of a
university under occupation.
Paperback: 978-1-78279-637-4 ebook: 978-1-78279-636-7

**Ghosts of My Life**
Writings on Depression, Hauntology and Lost Futures
Mark Fisher
Paperback: 978-1-78099-226-6 ebook: 978-1-78279-624-4

**Sweetening the Pill**
or How We Got Hooked on Hormonal Birth Control
Holly Grigg-Spall
Has contraception liberated or oppressed women?
*Sweetening the Pill* breaks the silence on the dark side of hormonal
contraception.
Paperback: 978-1-78099-607-3 ebook: 978-1-78099-608-0

**Why Are We The Good Guys?**
Reclaiming Your Mind from the Delusions of Propaganda
David Cromwell
A provocative challenge to the standard ideology that Western
power is a benevolent force in the world.
Paperback: 978-1-78099-365-2 ebook: 978-1-78099-366-9

**The Writing on the Wall**
On the Decomposition of Capitalism and its Critics
Anselm Jappe, Alastair Hemmens
A new approach to the meaning of social emancipation.
Paperback: 978-1-78535-581-3 ebook: 978-1-78535-582-0

## Enjoying It
Candy Crush and Capitalism
Alfie Bown
A study of enjoyment and of the enjoyment of studying. Bown asks what enjoyment says about us and what we say about enjoyment, and why.
Paperback: 978-1-78535-155-6 ebook: 978-1-78535-156-3


## Color, Facture, Art and Design
Iona Singh
This materialist definition of fine-art develops guidelines for architecture, design, cultural-studies and ultimately social change.
Paperback: 978-1-78099-629-5 ebook: 978-1-78099-630-1


## Neglected or Misunderstood
The Radical Feminism of Shulamith Firestone
Victoria Margree
An interrogation of issues surrounding gender, biology, sexuality, work and technology, and the ways in which our imaginations continue to be in thrall to ideologies of maternity and the nuclear family.
Paperback: 978-1-78535-539-4 ebook: 978-1-78535-540-0


## How to Dismantle the NHS in 10 Easy Steps (Second Edition)
Youssef El-Gingihy
The story of how your NHS was sold off and why you will have to buy private health insurance soon. A new expanded second edition with chapters on junior doctors' strikes and government blueprints for US-style healthcare.
Paperback: 978-1-78904-178-1 ebook: 978-1-78904-179-8

**Digesting Recipes**
The Art of Culinary Notation
Susannah Worth
A recipe is an instruction, the imperative tone of the expert, but
this constraint can offer its own kind of potential. A recipe need
not be a domestic trap but might instead offer escape – something
to fantasise about or aspire to.
Paperback: 978-1-78279-860-6 ebook: 978-1-78279-859-0

Most titles are published in paperback and as an ebook.
Paperbacks are available in traditional bookshops. Both print and
ebook formats are available online.
Follow us on Facebook
at https://www.facebook.com/ZeroBooks
and Twitter at https://twitter.com/Zer0Books